W9-AHE-962

Eucharist

Exploring the Diamond of Our Faith

DENNIS J. BILLY, C.Ss.R.

TWENTY-THIRD PUBLICATIONS
185 WILLOW STREET • PO BOX 180 • MYSTIC, CT 06355
TEL: 1-800-321-0411 • FAX: 1-800-572-0788
Bayard E-MAIL: ttpubs@aol.com • www.twentythirdpublications.com

Dedication

In loving memory of my Godmother,
Marie Piro (1927-2001)

Twenty-Third Publications
A Division of Bayard
185 Willow Street
P.O. Box 180
Mystic, CT 06355
(860) 536-2611 or (800) 321-0411
www.twentythirdpublications.com
ISBN:1-58595-359-8

Copyright ©2004 Dennis Billy, C.Ss.R. Permission is given to reproduce these pages as needed for non-commercial use in schools, churches, and other prayer groups. Otherwise, no part of this publication may be reproduced in any manner without prior written permission of the publisher. Write to the Permissions Editor.

Library of Congress Catalog Card Number: 2004106291
Printed in the U.S.A.

The Scripture passages contained herein are from the *New Revised Standard Version of the Bible*, copyright © 1989, by the Division of Christian Education of the National Council of Churches in the U.S.A. All rights reserved.

I AM ALL AT ONCE WHAT CHRIST IS,

'SINCE HE WAS WHAT I AM, AND

THIS JACK, JOKE, POOR POTSHERD,

'PATCH, MATCHWOOD, IMMORTAL DIAMOND,

IS IMMORTAL DIAMOND.

—Gerard Manley Hopkins

Acknowledgments

Parts of this book were previously published as: "Feeding the Multitude: Confronting the Mystery of Jesus," *Emmanuel* 108 (no. 2, 2002): 68-78 [Facet One]; "The Lord's Prayer and the Eucharist," *Emmanuel* 108 (no. 7, 2002): 400-9 [Facet Two]; "The Eucharist and Mark's Institution Narrative," *Spirituality Review* (Lent/Easter, 2003): 6-15 [Facet Three]; "The Road to Emmaus: The Journey of Discipleship," *Emmanuel* 107 (no. 3, 2001): 155-59, 163-64 [Facet Four]; "Eucharistic Faith: Jesus' Discourse on the Bread of Life," *Review for Religious* 61 (no. 6, 2002): 640-48 [Facet Five]; "Washing the Disciples' Feet (John 13:1–20): Eucharist and the Call to Service," *Emmanuel* 107 (no. 9, 2001): 522-29 [Facet Six]; "Eucharistic Encounter: A Meditative Reading of John 21:1–23," *Emmanuel* 107 (no. 4, 2001): 203-10, 223 [Facet Seven]; "Discipleship in the Primitive Church: A Look at Acts 2:42," *Emmanuel* 108 (no. 10, 2002): 580-90 [Facet Eight]; "Healing a Divided Community: The Institution Narrative of 1 Corinthians 11:23–25," *Emmanuel* 108 (no. 6, 2002): 324-332, 340 [Facet Nine]; "The Eucharist and the Body of Christ: A Reading of 1 Corinthians 12:12–31," *Emmanuel* 109 (no. 2, 2003): 68-78 [Facet Ten]. In keeping with the book's popular tone, footnotes have been kept to a minimum. The strictly exegetical material in the book represents mainstream New Testament scholarship, is not original to the author, and is generally held as common exegetical knowledge. Those interested in pursuing particular points of interest can begin by looking to such introductory manuals and reference works as Raymond Brown's *An Introduction to the New Testament* (New York: Doubleday, 1997) and *The New Jerome Biblical Commentary*, eds. Raymond E. Brown, Joseph E. Fitzmyer, and Roland E. Murphy (London, Geoffrey Chapman, 1989).

A word of thanks goes to Paul Bernier, S.S.S., editor of *Emmanuel* magazine, and to David L. Fleming, S.J., editor of *Review for Religious* and *Spirituality Review* for their permission to republish these essays in book form. A special word of thanks goes to Dan Connors of Twenty-Third Publications for his keen exegetical eye and invaluable editorial assistance.

Contents

Introduction

Have you ever gazed upon a finely cut diamond? Each of its many facets captures the sun in a slightly different way and reflects it outwardly with a dancing brilliance that dazzles the eye. Their combined effect sparks the imagination and brings out the inner beauty of both the beholder and the beheld. We wear diamonds—on our wrists, our fingers, around our necks—because we consider them precious. We want them to reflect not only the light of the sun, but also the light within our souls. We see in them something of the elegance, grace, and charm that we ourselves long to possess. Diamonds are beautiful; we long to be the same. The gift of a diamond says something of the beauty that one person sees in another.

The Eucharist is a diamond, an immortal diamond. One would not think so by merely taking part in it. It is a simple ritual that uses bread and wine in an act of common worship. To see the connection we must try to look beneath appearances. When pondered in the light of faith, this simple act of worship contains many facets, each of which reveals to us something about ourselves, as well as the mystery of the divine. Like a diamond, the Eucharist transforms the light it receives into something of even greater beauty: bread and wine, humble fruit of the earth and the sweat of human hands, become the body and blood of Christ. We cannot see this brilliant transformation taking place—at least not of our own accord. We see this change occurring only through the eyes of faith.

The Eucharist reflects the brilliance of the risen Lord. That brilliance enters our midst and into our bodies whenever we celebrate this sacrament. This communion with the Lord brings out of our own inner beauty a brilliance that we share by virtue of our being adopted sons and daughters of God. When we receive this sacrament we are given the opportunity to get in touch with our true identity. Through it we can recognize how much God has given us and how much we need to be thankful for. The word "Eucharist" itself comes from *eucharistia*, the Greek term for "thanks-giving." When we gather to break bread around the table of the Lord, we do so to give thanks to the Father in, with, and through the person of Jesus Christ. This action of thanksgiving makes sense only in the light of the gospel message. Outside of that context the Eucharist is not a priceless gem, but an empty ritual devoid of meaning and with no lasting value.

The early Christians knew that, in the Eucharist, their Lord had left with them a precious diamond. He gave them this mysterious gift because of the hidden beauty he saw deep within their hearts. Those same hearts burned within when they broke bread together and recognized his passing presence in their midst (see Lk 24:32). As a result of this experience, they became keenly aware of the intimate connection between the breaking of the bread and the life, death, and resurrection of Jesus Christ. The stories they told recount the various facets of this close, intimate relationship. Jesus' sayings, the narratives of his passion and death, and the stories of his post-resurrection appearances were first handed down at small Christian gatherings where they remembered the Lord Jesus and recognized his presence in the breaking of the bread.

When gathering these sources and incorporating them into their own accounts, the New Testament authors gave the Eucharist a central role in their presentation of the Christian faith. They did so not only with explicit references to its institution by Christ, but also through a variety of images and motifs that could be properly understood only against the backdrop of the eucharistic celebrations, during which the stories and teachings of Jesus were originally shared. The Eucharist, for them, was like a multifaceted diamond that reflected the light of Christ in many directions. This light brought out the inner beauty of the believing community and constantly reminded it of what it was and what it was called to do.

This book approaches the Eucharist as one would gaze upon the brilliance of a multifaceted diamond. It examines some of the most important passages of the New Testament related to the breaking of the bread in the light of such early Christian themes as discipleship, faith, prayer, celebration, healing, community, mystery, and service. Each of the texts presented here may be likened to a single facet of a diamond. Taken from the four gospels, the Acts of the Apostles, and the letters of St. Paul, they are all given a sound exegetical foundation and presented in a popular, easy-to-read style. Pertinent observations within each chapter, as well as a series of carefully planned reflection questions at the end, also help us to consider the significance of the Eucharist for our daily lives. The aim in all of this is to allow the light of faith to shine on the Eucharist so that we might behold the brilliance of the risen Lord and his presence in the believing community, his body, the church.

As with a diamond, it really does not matter which facet of the eucharistic mystery we focus on first. To have some order in our presentation, however, we have decided to follow the sequence of their appearance in the New Testament itself. Facets one through four treat material from the Synoptic Gospels (Matthew, Mark, and Luke). Facets five through seven examine some key passages from the Gospel of John. Facet eight looks at a text from the Acts of the Apostles, while facets nine and ten focus on elements in the Pauline corpus, specifically from Paul's first letter to the Corinthians.

There are two reasons for ordering the material in this manner. In the first place, doing so conveys a strong sense of the centrality of the Eucharist in some of the major components of the New Testament. Along with baptism, breaking bread together was a formative and defining characteristic of the nascent faith. Without it a community could hardly refer to itself as Christian, let alone a gathering of Jesus' disciples or an assembly of the faithful.

Second, the variety and repetition of themes by the New Testament authors affirm both the richness of their eucharistic teaching and its pervasive presence in the constituent traditions involved in the emergence, growth, and diffusion of the Christian spiritual tradition. Each of the chapters reflects not one, but several dimensions of the eucharistic mystery that surface in other literary contexts and for different ends. It is hoped that, as with a finely cut diamond, the combined effect of these chapters will reflect the light of the New Testament faith in a way any one of them could do only in part and with more limited effect.

While the book does not claim to present a comprehensive treatment of the scriptural foundations of the church's eucharistic teaching, it covers enough ground to offer a good sense of how the early Christians viewed

Jesus' Last Supper with his disciples as a defining moment in his life that both permitted and sustained their own sharing in his paschal mystery. Like the reflections of the sun in a finely cut diamond, it seeks to reveal an inner beauty that sparks our imaginations and resonates within our hearts. As such, it seeks to deepen our understanding of the Eucharist and inspire us to probe those areas of belief that we still find difficult to accept. It should also encourage us to bring our problems and concerns to our celebration of the Eucharist in a way similar to that of Jesus' earliest followers. Doing so on a regular basis will inevitably draw us closer to Jesus and gradually deepen our desire to reflect the light of his love within our hearts to those we meet.

Confronting a Mystery

Jesus Feeds the Multitude

Taking the five loaves and the two fish, he looked up to heaven, and blessed and broke the loaves, and gave them to his disciples to set before the people; and he divided the two fish among them all. And all ate and were filled; and they took up twelve baskets full of broken pieces and of the fish. Those who had eaten the loaves numbered five thousand men. (Mk 6:41–44)

I have always had a difficult time with the gospel stories of Jesus feeding the multitude. They seem too far removed from ordinary human experience to be taken at face value. Multiplying loaves and fish to feed a cast of thousands is hard to envision. Where did these extra loaves and fish come from? Who put them there? Did they simply appear out of nowhere? Does faith in Jesus require suspending one's belief in the laws of nature? I certainly hope not.

When reading these accounts I often find myself reacting to them with a strange mixture of childlike trust and deep-seated suspicion. It would be nice to believe that Jesus could perform such miracles, but his doing so would create as many problems as it would solve. Why, for example, would God intervene in human affairs on this particular occasion and not in the many other situations of intense hunger that have plagued humanity throughout its history? Does not such selective generosity reflect a degree of indifference (perhaps even cruelty) in God? If not, then how else can we explain God's unwillingness to step in on our behalf in other equally (perhaps even more) urgent and needy cases? I have mixed reactions when confronted with these stories. I feel pulled in opposite directions: wanting to believe yet somehow holding back. I wish I could have been there to judge whatever happened for myself.

Despite these difficulties, the stories of Jesus feeding the multitude still excite the imagination and lead us to ponder the power of Jesus' presence in our midst. When reading them I often try to place myself in the scene as an active participant in the unfolding drama rather than as a detached and distant onlooker. Doing so helps me to place my suspicions aside so that the deep spiritual meaning of these stories can rise to the surface, engage me in the present moment, and penetrate my heart. Reading them in this way does not answer all my questions—not by a long shot. Doing so, however, raises different, more important questions for me about Jesus' identity and mission. These stories confront me with the mystery of Christ and his power to feed my deep inner hungers. Once these are satisfied, whatever other misgivings I may have about the validity of the accounts move to the background or gently fall into place.

The Bare Bones

The account of Jesus feeding the multitude appears six times in the gospels: twice in Matthew (14:15–21; 15:32–39), twice in Mark (6:34–44; 8:1–10), and once each in both Luke (9:10–17) and John (6:1–15). No other gospel episode comes close to this high number of occurrences. The frequency of its appearance in these sacred texts attests to both its popularity and its importance for the early Christian community. Although each of the gospel writers emphasizes different elements of the story to support his particular theological vision, all of them employ the same narrative substructure and a number of themes fundamental to the early Christian kerygma. Although it is impossible to determine what exactly happened at this important crossroad of Jesus' Galilean ministry, the event clearly made a deep impression on his followers, one that they would look back to time and again as a turning point in Jesus' life and mission.

As narrated by the evangelists, the basic plot of these accounts is simple and easy to distill. Aside from some minor discrepancies in detail, the underlying substructure of the narratives remains fundamentally the same. A large crowd follows Jesus to an out-of-the-way place, where he teaches them at length. Late in the day a request comes that he should send the crowd away so that they can find food to eat. Jesus suggests that the disciples use their own resources to feed the crowd. They respond that they cannot feed such a large group with only a few loaves of bread and some fish. Jesus then instructs his disciples to have the people rest on the ground. He then takes the bread and fish, looks up to heaven, blesses them, breaks them, and distributes them. The people eat until they have had enough, and the disciples collect an abundance of leftover food.

The accounts differ in such details as the size of the gathering, the dialogue between Jesus and his disciples, the number of loaves and fish, the way the people rest on the ground, the manner of distribution, and the number of baskets of leftovers collected. They agree, however, on the basic elements of the story and are unanimous in their perception that what took place was a convincing display of Jesus' prodigious power. The more common title of the account, "The Multiplication of the Loaves and Fish," emphasizes this prominent feature of the event.

Interpreting the Event

When going through the various accounts of this episode we need to remember that the evangelists were not trying to write a "history" in the modern sense of the term. The gospels are first and foremost documents of faith. Such a statement does not mean that they do not contain historical evidence or that the evangelists were deliberately trying to distort "the facts" of a particular event. It only means that they were trying to express in words what they had discovered about the meaning and message of Jesus of Nazareth.

All of their memories of his historical life were filtered through their experience of him in the Christ event: their encounter of Jesus in his passion, death, and resurrection influenced their understanding of his public ministry and affected the way they presented their recollection of him. We must also remember that modern science today tends to discount the notion of an objective truth (historical or otherwise) existing independently from our capacity to observe it. We influence what we observe just as much as we are influenced by it, if not more. Historical truth is always an interpretation of one's experience of what happened. While some interpretations may be determined to be more satisfactory than others, the most we can ever arrive at is an interpretation of what occurred.

In light of the above, the various discrepancies in the six accounts of Jesus feeding the multitude can be explained not only by the different theological aims of the evangelists, but also by different perceptions of the eyewitnesses themselves. Did the disciples have five loaves and two fish or seven loaves and a few small fish? Did they have twelve baskets left over or only seven? Were there five thousand present that day or only four? Did the number include the women and children present—or not? Rather than explaining these differences away by maintaining that Jesus fed the multitudes on at least two separate occasions (hence the duplicate versions preserved in the gospels of Matthew and Mark), we can simplify matters by saying that what occurred was perceived differently by those present and handed down orally as different traditions. These traditions were eventually written and made their way into the gospel narratives as two separate occurrences. Today most exegetes generally agree with this simpler explanation of the event.

A Look to Elisha

In addition to different perceptions of what took place, it makes perfect sense that the evangelists would have looked to the Hebrew Scriptures for certain points of reference to help them mold the account of Jesus' feeding of the multitude into an appropriate narrative shape. For them, doing so would not be a falsification of what happened in that deserted place near the end of Jesus' ministry in Galilee, but an even deeper affirmation of it.

In the present instance, the accounts in question bear a remarkable resemblance to the following story of the prophet Elisha's multiplication of the loaves in 2 Kings 4:42–44:

A man came from Baal-shalishah, bringing food from the first fruits to the man of God: twenty loaves of barley and fresh ears of grain in his sack. Elisha said, "Give it to the people and let them eat." But his servant said, "How can I set this before a hundred people?" So he repeated, "Give it to the people and let them eat, for thus says the Lord, 'They shall eat and have some left.'" He set it before them, they ate, and had some left, according to the word of the Lord.

According to Reginald Fuller, this story from the Elisha cycle (2 Kings 2:1–8:29) serves as "the literary prototype" of the various gospel accounts of Jesus feeding the multitude. All follow the same basic pattern found in this very brief story: "(1) food is brought to the man of God; (2) the amount of food is specified; (3) it is objected that the quantity is inadequate; (4) behaving as master of the situation the man of God ignores the objection and commands the food to be distributed; (5) the crowd not only have enough to eat, but there was some left."[1]

The benefit to shaping the account of Jesus' feeding of the multitude after Elisha's multiplication of the loaves is plain. Elisha took up the mantle of Elijah and succeeded him as the Lord's prophet. By adopting this narrative substructure, the sacred authors depict Jesus as the New Elijah who speaks the Word of God to God's people and performs wonderful feats on their behalf. When seen in this light, Jesus' feeding of the multitude takes on the dimensions of a prophetic action. As an authentic utterance of the Word of God, this action points beyond itself and actually brings into effect what it symbolizes. From this perspective the event can easily be understood as a foreshadowing of the Eucharist, a meal that itself is considered a foretaste of the messianic banquet.

The New Moses

Another Old Testament figure whose story influences the interpretation of the account of Jesus feeding the multitude is Moses. Unlike the Elisha story, which provides the narrative substructure for the gospel accounts, the connection between Moses and Jesus as the New Moses comes about by the placement of individual accounts within the larger gospel narra-

---

1. *Preaching the New Lectionary* (Collegevill, Minn.: The Liturgical Press, 1974), 406.

tives. Although a parallel between the Exodus account of the manna from heaven and the multiplication of the loaves would be easy enough to draw, this typology does not figure greatly in the actual text of the multiplication accounts themselves. To find the connection between Moses and Jesus, one has to study the accounts of the feeding of the multitude in their larger literary contexts.

Moses, the great prophet and lawgiver of the Jewish people, was also the instrument of many miraculous interventions, most notable of which was his parting of the Red Sea (Ex 14:10–22). Among the miracles he performed during their forty years of wandering in the desert were those of the manna and quail (Ex 16:1–15) and the drawing of water from the rock (Ex 17:1–7). In both instances, Moses served as intercessor for his people, hearing their bickering and quarrelsome complaints, bringing them to God, and then acting as the Lord's chosen instrument. If God had not intervened through him in these miraculous ways, Moses would have lost his authority over his people and they would have continued to wander without direction in the desert of Sinai.

The comparison with Jesus is most telling. While Moses could command the sea and provide his people with food and water, the evangelists have Jesus performing similar and even more astounding feats. When he feeds the multitude, he does not provide his hungry listeners with a mere wafer-like substance that appeared as "a fine flaky substance, as fine as frost on the ground" (Ex 16:14), but multiplies real bread to fill and satisfy their empty stomachs. In three of the accounts, he walks on water immediately after feeding the multitude (see Mt 14:22–33; Mk 6:45–52; Jn 6:16–24), a much more marvelous event than merely drawing water from a rock or even parting a sea so that one could walk through it. In the Gospel of Luke, the account of the Jesus calming the storm (Lk 8:22–25) occurs in close proximity to the miracle of the loaves and fish (Lk 9:10–17). These miracles performed by Jesus in his own name far exceed anything by Moses for his people in God's name.

By all counts, Jesus is the New Moses, the prophet of the New Covenant. The episode of the multiplication of the loaves and fishes evokes Moses' miracle of the manna and quail—and far surpasses it. John's gospel makes this connection explicit in Jesus' discourse on the Bread of Life (Jn 6:25–59), which appears immediately after the accounts of Jesus feeding the multitude (Jn 6:1–15) and walking on water (Jn 6:16–24). The Synoptic Gospels make the same connection by placing the account of the transfiguration (Mt 17:1–8; Mk 9:2–8; Lk 9:28–36) in close proximity to the multiplication miracles. High atop the mountain of the transfiguration, Jesus converses with Moses and Elijah because he continues their mission to God's people and brings it to fulfillment. The accounts of the multiplication of the loaves and fish reinforce this point by virtue of the narrative substructure they follow and the larger literary context in which they are placed.

Eucharistic Symbolism

In addition to the Old Testament figures of Elisha and Moses, the primitive Christian community also allowed their celebration of the Eucharist to guide their interpretation of Jesus' feeding of the multitude. The accounts are filled with the symbols and language of the eucharistic liturgy: "reclining" or "sitting down," "taking the loaves," "blessing the bread," "breaking it," "giving it," "eating it"—to name but a few. Jesus' request, moreover, that the crowd break up into small groups reflects the intimate atmosphere of the early domestic churches prevalent in the early years of Christian missionary expansion when local church membership was still relatively small. We should keep in mind that the early Christians looked not only to the Last Supper as the basis for the eucharistic celebration, but also to their mealtime fellowship with Jesus both during his lifetime and in his post-resurrectional appearances. It was quite natural for them, therefore, to weave eucharistic imagery and symbolism into accounts of their humble yet refreshing repasts with the Lord.

When interpreted in the light of the early Christian liturgy, the accounts of Jesus feeding the multitude become a concrete foreshadowing of the Eucharist. It is interesting to note, however, that the sacrificial aspect of the meal—the connection between the Last Supper and Calvary—is not heavily emphasized. This is so possibly because the priestly nature of Jesus' commemorative meal and its close relationship to his sacrificial death may not have surfaced yet in the awareness of the believing community. That is not to say that this intrinsic relationship did not exist at the time and is therefore nothing but a later doctrinal accretion, but that the believing community had simply not yet come to an understanding of the full significance of the breaking of the bread. In the accounts of Jesus feeding the multitude, the pervading eucharistic imagery points much more forcefully to the celebration of the messianic banquet. The division into groups of hundreds and fifties (see Mk 6:40; Lk 9:14) and the abundant leftovers (Mt 14:20; 15:37; Mk 5:43; 8:8; Lk 9:17; Jn 6:13) point to the bountiful refreshment that will take place at such a meal.

The eucharistic symbolism permeating these accounts also allows the liturgical nature of the gospel texts themselves to come to light. These narratives were put together not for private devotion, but to be read aloud during a community celebration. This important liturgical context provides yet another reason for seeing in the multiplication of the loaves and fish a foreshadowing in the life of Jesus of the meal that he asked his disciples to celebrate in his memory. The eucharistic symbolism in the accounts helps the believing community to identify more closely with the action of Jesus that is taking place before them. Just as Jesus performed the miracle of the loaves and fish, they are invited—through the symbols in the text and in the action in which they are presently participating—to behold another miracle that will soon take place in the breaking of the bread. When seen in this light, the accounts of Jesus feeding the multitude help the believing community to enter more deeply into eucharistic celebration. What Jesus performed in a very visible and physical way during his public ministry is now being realized even more powerfully (albeit invisibly) in the breaking of the bread.

Reflection

As with most miracle stories, the accounts of Jesus feeding the multitudes bring us face to face with what we believe. While we will never be able to determine what exactly took place on that occasion, we know that it impressed Jesus' followers strongly enough to record it more than any other gospel story.

When confronted with these miracle stories, however, many of us give in to the tendency to explain them away by means of some natural occurrence. In the case of the multiplication of the loaves and fish, the most common explanation is that Jesus performed a miracle not of nature but of the heart. According to this scenario, as the crowd saw Jesus' disciples sharing what little they had with others, their hearts were so moved that they opened their own haversacks and began to do the same.

The proponents of this interpretation argue that it would have been highly unlikely for so many people to follow Jesus into such a deserted, out-of-the-way place with no provisions of any kind. Moved by the example of Jesus and his disciples, the crowd was able to feed itself from its own resources. So great was this action of mass sharing that everyone was filled to satisfaction and many leftovers were collected.

This explanation of the multiplication of the loaves remains popular in some corners. Unwilling to accept the possibility of divine intervention of any sort, some exegetes find in this explanation a feasible way of explaining the details of the accounts without having to admit the presence and action of a supernatural power.

The problem with this explanation, however, is that it explains away too much. Although it is true that Jesus could have affected a change of heart in so many people without a miraculous display of power, such an interpretation undermines our trust in his ability to do otherwise. Jesus' multiplication of the loaves and fish, and the manner in which he did it, has a direct bearing on the mysterious nature of his identity. Although the natural interpretation of the event may satisfy our rational doubts and uncertainties, it evades too easily the episode's central focus.

The accounts of Jesus feeding the multitude bring us face to face with the mystery of Christ. To deprive these accounts of the miraculous deflates the significance they had in the primitive Christian community and diminishes our own understanding of the power and glory of Christ. Doing so means that we place more trust in the power of reason (and a very limited notion of it, at that) than in the person of Jesus. The very purpose of these gospel accounts, however, is to increase our trust in Jesus' role as the prophet of the New Covenant and host of the messianic banquet. If the line is not drawn somewhere, the attitude supporting this natural interpretation of Jesus feeding the multitude will influence other elements of the gospel narrative, even the resurrection. Once the miracle has been taken out of Christianity, we will be left with nothing but an empty doctrinal shell devoid of any real power to initiate the reign of God in the world.

Conclusion

To be honest, most of us probably have ambivalent feelings toward the various accounts of Jesus feeding the multitude. I know I do. A part of us wants to believe in the miracle as it is told by the gospel writers; another part of us is skeptical about miracles in general and of this kind in particular.

The multiplication of the loaves and fish seems to contradict all that we were ever taught about the laws of nature. We wonder where our faith will lead us if we suspend skepticism in this instance and allow for a divine exception. At the same time, Christian belief tells us that God created the universe out of nothing and continues to hold it in being. If this basic tenet of the faith is true, then it seems quite rational to conclude that an all-powerful creator could just as easily produce something out of something (bread from bread).

Our problem with the account of Jesus feeding the multitude is that it puts us in touch with a fundamental conflict in our belief system. We find ourselves, at one and the same time, both believing it and disbelieving it, hoping in its truth, yet somehow in touch with an underground current of doubt telling us that it could not possibly be so. Through this difficult and quite precarious "coincidence of opposites," the accounts provide us with the unique opportunity to plumb the depths of our faith and to examine the assumptions supporting it.

As we go about doing so, we should realize that such struggles regarding the possibility of divine intervention were largely foreign to the world of the primitive Christian community. What came easily to them comes to us only with great difficulty and much prayer. In either case, when reading these accounts believers from both worlds ultimately come up against the same unfolding reality in their lives—an existential encounter with the unfathomable mystery of Christ.

Reflection Questions

• What do you find believable in the accounts of Jesus feeding the multitude? What do you find difficult to accept? What criteria do you use for determining what is believable or not?

• Do you believe in miracles? What is your attitude toward the possibility of divine intervention in the world? In what way does this attitude shape your interpretation of these accounts?

• What were the gospel authors trying to say through the accounts of the multiplication of the loaves and fish? Is their message still fresh? Does it need to be adapted in any way?

• In what way does Jesus follow in the footsteps of the prophets Elisha and Moses? In what way does he transcend them?

• In what way do these accounts confront you with the mystery of Jesus? What do they lead you to affirm or reject about his identity?

Learning to Pray

The Lord's Prayer

Our Father, who art in heaven, hallowed be thy name; thy kingdom come; thy will be done on earth as it is in heaven. Give us this day our daily bread; and forgive us our trespasses as we forgive those who trespass against us; and lead us not into temptation, but deliver us from evil. (Matthew 6:9–13, as it appears in the Roman Missal)

The words of the Lord's Prayer are deeply embedded in my memory. Not a day goes by without my praying them. I cannot remember how or when I learned them. It seems like they have always been quietly resting in my mind, just waiting to be summoned up for easy recall. Sometimes I think they got there without my even knowing it. Frequent repetition and constant exposure to the church's eucharistic liturgy have made them steady and stalwart companions to my prayer. To my mind, they are among the most beautiful words in all of Scripture—and also the most familiar. It is hard for me to imagine their absence from my life.

Jesus taught his disciples to pray in this way, and that is just fine with me. He encourages us to make his words our own. When we do so, our voices blend with his and our hearts open up to our Father in heaven. The Lord's Prayer is a special gift from God to God's special people. It is Jesus' prayer and the prayer of his body, the church. It is the prayer of Christian discipleship, one that points us in the right direction, sets us on our way, and helps us to stay the course. Jesus gave us this prayer so that we could share in his intimate relationship with his Father. Through it he affirms his love for us, embraces us as his brothers and sisters, and reveals the truth of our divine adoption.

For reasons such as these, the "Our Father" is often referred to as the Christian prayer par excellence. Rooted in the words and expressions of Jesus himself, it appears at two places in the gospel narratives (Mt 6:9–13; Lk 11:2–4) and has been reworked by the evangelists to express their specific theological concerns and interests. Although it can be prayed in private (and at least one gospel writer encourages us to voice it in this way, see Mt 6:5–6), it also has a strong communal focus and has gained a prominent place in the church's eucharistic worship. Jesus taught his disciples to address the God of Israel as "Abba, Father." The Lord's Prayer is a testament to this fundamental teaching and presents us with a simple way of asserting this revolutionary way of relating to God.

The Lucan Account

Of the two versions, the one in Luke's gospel probably corresponds more closely to the wording and form that appeared in the so-called Q source, an earlier but now lost written document from which the authors of Matthew and Luke are said to have drawn much of their non-Marcan material. Both authors probably had access to this earlier document and based their presentation of the Lord's Prayer on what they found there. Since Matthew's version of the prayer is longer and more highly stylized, it is commonly thought to have undergone more editing than the shorter and simpler account found in Luke. For this reason, Luke's version is generally thought to correspond more faithfully to the earlier written source upon which it is based and hence to provide closer access to the original setting of the prayer and possibly even to the actual words used by Jesus himself.

Most Christians are not as familiar with Luke's account, because Matthew's version is by far the more poetic and has become the version used in both public worship and private devotion. The simple, more straightforward account from Luke's gospel reads thus:

He was praying in a certain place, and after he had finished, one of his disciples said to him, "Lord, teach us to pray, as John taught his disciples." He said to them, "When you pray, say:

Father,

hallowed be your name,

your kingdom come.

Give us each day our daily bread.

And forgive us our sins

for we ourselves forgive everyone indebted to us.

And do not bring us to the time of trial." (Lk 11:1–4)

As in Matthew, Luke's version of the prayer begins with Jesus addressing God with the familiar designation of "Father." This intimate form of address was unusual for the Jews of Jesus' day, who were normally forbidden to utter God's name lest they use it in vain or offend God's holiness. Jesus takes the exact opposite approach and encourages his followers to do likewise. God, for him, is a loving father and should be approached with an open and loving heart.

After the opening appellation, Luke's version has five petitions (as opposed to six in Matthew). These petitions ask: (1) that God's name be hallowed, (2) that his kingdom come, (3) that he provide those praying with daily bread, (4) that he forgive them their sins, and (5) that he not subject them to the trial. The fourth petition is expanded to imply that God will not forgive us our sins if we do not forgive those who have injured us. Although it is not as apparent as in Matthew's version, the communal emphasis of the prayer comes through in the use of the plural form rather than the singular in the third, fourth, and fifth petitions.

The Lucan Setting

The setting in which Luke's account takes place also has special significance. Unlike Matthew's version, which appears at a central place in Jesus' Sermon on the Mount (Mt 5–7), Luke's takes place in a more private setting where the disciples, after observing Jesus at prayer, ask him to teach them how to pray (Lk 11:1). One may wonder how such a simple question could come from the lips of grown men who lived in a religious culture that placed great emphasis on the observance of the Law and the various rituals and prayers included in it. Did they not already know how to pray? Had they not been taught the official prayers of Jewish observance from an early age? What was missing in their traditional forms of prayer that led them to ask this question?

The answer lies in the second part of their request: "Teach us to pray, as John taught his disciples." John the Baptist's preaching and prophetic action had such a strong effect in his day that it inspired a small but clearly identifiable movement on the religious horizon of early first-century Palestine. The leaders of such movements often provided their followers with a distinctive way of praying. In this respect, the Baptist was no exception.

By posing this question to Jesus, his followers voice their desire to be explicitly identified as his disciples and to submit their relationship with God to his oversight. They have observed Jesus at prayer from a distance long enough. They now want him to teach them what he knows about prayer so that they can share in his intimate knowledge of God. Jesus responds with a few simple phrases that even a child could remember. By teaching them how to pray in this way, he gives his disciples a deeper insight into what it means to follow him. Luke intends Jesus' words to be seen as the prayer of Christian discipleship. Being a disciple, for him, means praying with childlike trust, and loving the way Jesus does—with one's whole heart, mind, soul, and strength. The words of the Lord's Prayer are nothing but a vehicle allowing this to happen. What matters most is the interior disposition with which one voices them.

Learning to Pray

The situation in which Luke places his version of the Lord's Prayer has special relevance for those of us who seek to walk the path of Christian discipleship today. We too have observed Jesus from a distance, not of physical space as in the case of his earliest followers, but of historical time. We too wish to learn from him so that we can plumb the depths of our hearts and grow in intimacy with the Father. We too need to ask the question: "Lord, teach us to pray, as John taught his disciples." In doing so, however, we must seek much more than just the right terms and phrases.

The words of the "Our Father" have been repeated so often and have become so familiar to us that, for many, they have lost much of their original force and sense of urgency. Jesus offered his disciples a radically different way of relating to God, one so liberating that even the Baptist sent his followers to inquire about the nature of his identity (see Lk 7:18–23). By addressing God as "Abba, Father," Jesus recast the manner in which God and humanity conversed. The basis of this relationship was not one of fear and trepidation, but of intimacy, closeness, and loving involvement.

When asking Jesus to teach us how to pray, we need to break open the words he has given us and rediscover the attitudes of heart, mind, and soul that he intended should be behind the words we voice. When Jesus taught his disciples to pray, he did much more than give them a simple prayer that could be memorized and eventually given out by rote. He taught them how to pray by doing so in front of them, not off in the distance where his intimate relationship with the Father could not be observed. It was the experience of actually seeing Jesus praying to the Father before their eyes that touched the disciples so deeply and convinced them of its great relevance for their lives.

Our task is to recapture that moment in time through a creative act of imagination so that Jesus' words can touch us the way they did his disciples. For this to happen we must be willing to imagine ourselves in the very situation in which Jesus taught his disciples how to pray and to open ourselves to the hope that we too can share in such a relationship with God. This intimate relationship with his Father was what Jesus was offering his disciples—and it is precisely what he is offering us.

We need to do in our day and age what Matthew and Luke were trying to do in theirs. We must use the powers of the imagination to reconstruct in a balanced and creative way the circumstances surrounding the action of Jesus teaching his disciples how to pray. Only in this way will the words of his prayer have the same kind of impact on us that it had on them. The key to doing so is to remember that Jesus was demonstrating by his own example the disciples' need to address God as Father on every level of their being. To pray the "Our Father" in any other way compromises Jesus' words and diminishes the effect they have on our ongoing conversion.

The Dimensions of Human Existence

One helpful way of imagining the way Jesus taught his disciples to pray is to invoke the apostle Paul's understanding of the human person as an intimate unity of spirit, soul, and body (1 Th 5:23). Even though Jesus probably did not compose his prayer with these dimensions of human existence specifically in mind, his words reflect a deep sensitivity to the great variety of human needs and emphasize the importance of expressing them to God in prayer (see Lk 11:5–13). As one of the oldest anthropologies in the New Testament, Paul's presentation gives us some helpful clues about what it might mean for us to be in touch with these various needs and to express every dimension of our lives to God in prayer.

"Spirit" (*pneuma*), for Paul, stands for the innermost depths of the human person as it is open to the divine presence and awake to God's Spirit. It is that aspect of the person that communes with God beneath the sphere of human consciousness and cries out, "Abba, Father," from the depths of the human heart (Rom 8:15). In the Christian tradition this is the level of human existence that yearns for the direct experience of God in contemplative prayer. It is that dimension of the human person that seeks to pierce through all concepts of the nature of the Godhead and to encounter the ultimate ground of reality as it is.

"Soul" (*psyche*), for Paul, refers to the conscious, imaginative, and deliberative level of human existence. Here, reason and feeling play active roles in constructing the concepts upon which a positive theology of God is based. This dimension of human existence speaks to God through the images of mental prayer. Affective expressions of love, the examination of consciousness, resolutions to action, prayers of petition, and the meditative reading of Scripture all find a place in this important constituent aspect of the human person.

"Body" (*soma*), for Paul, refers to corporeal human existence, not in any denigrated sense (as when he contrasts spirit [*pneuma*] with flesh [*sarx*]), but as a neutral, albeit essential, element of human existence. It is the dimension of the person that, although under the sway of the "law of the flesh" (*sarx*), has been, is, and will be redeemed by those living according to the Spirit of Christ. Prayer seeks expression even on this, the most visible and concrete of all levels of human existence. It does so through vocal expression (e.g., singing, verbal meditations), symbols (e.g., the sign of the cross, uplifted arms, the holding of hands), posture (e.g., kneeling, standing, bowing one's head), and the rigors of corporeal sacrifice (e.g., fasting and abstinence).

As developed above, Paul's understanding of human existence and its implications for praying the Lord's Prayer should also be considered in conjunction with his understanding of the church as "The Body of Christ" (Eph 1:23; Col 1:18). Here, the social dimension of Pauline anthropology comes to the fore and highlights the communal orientation of each level of human existence. In other words, the contemplative, mental, and physical levels of human prayer reach their fullest expression only to the extent that they are done "in Christ" and, hence, in solidarity with all those who, in varying degrees, are incorporated into his body, the church. When seen in this light, the community of the church gathered around the table of the Lord represents the fullest expression of the human person at prayer. The contemplative, mental, corporeal, and social aspects of human existence come together at the liturgy, when the church and its members are most fully themselves in the presence of their God.

At the Table of the Lord

These insights from Paul remind us of the wide scope of human experience and of the importance of involving each of these dimensions—the spiritual, the mental, the corporeal, and the social—in our prayer. They also give us an insight into something of what Jesus' disciples must have experienced when their master shared with them his own way of praying to God. Jesus gave his disciples an example of someone whose being was totally absorbed in intimate conversation with the Father. Every level of his existence was opened up to God in prayer and completely immersed in the depths of God's Spirit. When seen from this perspective, the words of the prayer itself convey only a superficial understanding of what Jesus was trying to communicate to his disciples. Much more important was the attitude of childlike trust that enabled him to hold nothing back from the Father and to present his needs with the humble hope that he would be listened to and cared for.

These insights from Paul also help us to see the great importance placed on reciting the Lord's Prayer together when celebrating the Eucharist. At the close of the eucharistic prayer, the presbyter, acting in the person of Christ, invites us to pray to the Father using the words that Jesus, our Lord and Savior, has taught us. Praying the "Our Father" at this time, at the very summit of Christian worship and when the church is most fully itself, provides us with the opportunity to turn every dimension of our personal and corporate identity over to the Lord. At that moment, Christ is closer to us than he was even to his disciples when he taught them to pray and to call God "Abba, Father" so many years ago. By making the Lord's Prayer our own, we are united in an intimate way to the saving action of Christ that is taking place in our midst.

How is this so? As members of his body, the church, we pray through Christ, with Christ, and in Christ. Christ, in turn, prays through, with, and in us—all in the unity of the Spirit. By praying as the Lord has instructed us, we affirm our identity as disciples as we watch with eager longing for the coming of the kingdom. At the Eucharist the eschatological dimension of the prayer comes to the fore and takes on even greater significance. The Lord's kingdom touches every dimension of human existence. For this reason it is important that we involve every dimension of our lives in our prayer. By becoming absorbed in the prayer in this way, we affirm our claim to the fullness of redemption that Christ has gained for us and look forward to the time when the darkness of sin will be rooted out from every corner of our hearts. Christ, the Lord, has redeemed, is redeeming, and will redeem us on every level of our existence. Nothing lies outside the scope of his transforming grace. The Lord's Prayer affirms this fundamental truth of Christian existence and helps us to look with eager expectancy to the fulfillment of the Lord's promises in our lives. It does so by reminding us that Christ came to show us the way to the Father and that the relationship we are called to share with God is of the most intimate kind imaginable.

Conclusion
The Lord's Prayer is the Christian prayer par excellence. Although most of us are more familiar with the Matthean version, the one supplied by Luke displays less external influence and probably comes closer to the circum-

stances in which the Lord himself originally composed the prayer. Luke presents the prayer as Jesus' response to a query by his disciples about the way they should pray. It reminds us of the close relationship between prayer and the call to discipleship. It also reveals something of the intimate relationship we are called to share with God, our Father.

Although it can be prayed anywhere, the Lord's Prayer has a special place at the church's eucharistic worship. When it is gathered around the table of the Lord, the believing community is most fully itself and can express itself on many levels. When reciting it together, we should be conscious of the many dimensions of our human makeup: the physical, the mental, the spiritual, and the social. Doing so binds us more closely together as a believing community and helps us to understand the deeper significance of being brothers and sisters in the Lord. We can address God as "Abba, Father," only because of Jesus. He taught us to pray the way he did: simply, humbly, and straight from the heart. When at Eucharist, we join him in his prayer to the Father and celebrate the deep bond of love that joins us to him and to one another.

The Eucharist highlights the eschatological dimension of the Lord's Prayer. It does so by exhorting us to pray for the coming of the kingdom even as we celebrate the Lord's presence in our midst. This "already-but-not-yet" character of our worship helps us to look beneath the level of appearances and to profess the Lord's presence even in the midst of what we perceive as his absence. The Lord's Prayer bids us to place everything into the hands of the Father. Just as Jesus commended his life to him, so too are we called to trust in the power of love to help us overcome the trials that find us in life. Jesus taught his disciples to address God as "Father," to hallow his name, to pray for the coming of the kingdom, and to bring him their every need. He bids us to do likewise, to address God in this same revolutionary way—and to do so often.

Reflection Questions

• Do you find it easy to pray the Our Father? Do the words still have meaning for you?

• What does it mean to pray on every level of human existence? Have you ever prayed the Our Father in this way? Have you ever tried?

• Do you think of the Our Father as the prayer of Christian discipleship? What does the prayer ask of you? How does it challenge you?

• Do you find it easy to address God as "Abba, Father"? In what other ways would you like to address God?

• Do you prefer to pray the prayer in private or in common?

• Which version of the Our Father do you prefer, the one in Matthew or in Luke? What is the reason behind your preference? Which comes most easily to you when you imagine Jesus teaching his disciples how to pray?

Celebrating Eucharist

The Last Supper

While they were eating, he took a loaf of bread, and after blessing it he broke it, gave it to them, and said, "Take; this is my body." Then he took a cup, and after giving thanks he gave it to them, and all of them drank from it. He said to them, "This is my blood of the covenant, which is poured out for many. Truly I tell you, I will never again drink of the fruit of the vine until that day when I drink it new in the kingdom of God." (Mk 14:22–25)

If I could go back in time, one of the historical events that I would most like to visit would be Jesus' last meal with his disciples. I say this because the eucharistic celebration is so central to Christian worship that a better idea of what took place at its institution could not help but give us a deeper appreciation of its significance for the ongoing life of the church. To be there with Jesus when he first said the words of institution, to be able to look into his eyes, to watch his gestures, to listen to the intonations of his voice, and to share in the fellowship of that intimate gathering of disciples could only deepen our faith in the mysteries we celebrate when we break bread together.

Or would it? Being with Jesus at that particular moment offers no special guarantee that our relationship with him would be any deeper. Just look at those who were actually with him at the Last Supper. Most of them deserted him. One denied him not once, but three times. Another betrayed him and eventually killed himself. Who is to say that our reactions would be any different? Simply being with Jesus at that pivotal moment of his life does not mean that we would be any closer to him than we already are.

When all is said and done, what took place at the institution of the Eucharist can be truly appreciated only when seen through the eyes of faith. Being physically with Jesus as he celebrated his last meal with his disciples would benefit us only if we carried our faith along with us. Leave that behind and our journey through time to his side would be of little consequence. The narrative of Scripture and a heartfelt and prayerful understanding of its relation to our own lives would benefit us so very much more. A look at the account from the Gospel of Mark underscores this important interplay.

Of all the gospel accounts of the Last Supper, the one from Mark is the earliest and most straightforward. It is generally agreed that its style and choice of words point to an early liturgical tradition from Palestine, most likely from Jerusalem itself. It is also widely held to have served as the model for the other accounts in Matthew and Luke. Although it is not the earliest New Testament account of the institution narrative (Paul's account in 1 Cor 11:23–25 predates it), it is the first to be preserved in the larger context of the Passion narrative. Its place in this narrative reveals much about the way the early Christian community understood the Eucharist and its relevance to the Christ event. It has much to enlighten us about in our own journey of faith.

Overall Narrative Context

Mark's account of the institution of the Eucharist (Mk 14:22–25) is a small (albeit significant) part of a larger narrative that encompasses the events surrounding Jesus' passion, death, and resurrection. The framework of this narrative takes in the final three chapters of Mark's gospel (Mk 14–16) and provides a simple, straightforward description of what occurred. The major components of this narrative are as follows:

The conspiracy against Jesus (Mk 14:1–2)
The anointing at Bethany (Mk 14:3–9)

Judas betrays Jesus (Mk 14:10–11)
Preparations for the Passover supper (Mk 14:12–16)
The treachery of Judas foretold (Mk 14:17–21)
The institution of the Eucharist (Mk 14:22–25)
Peter's denial foretold (Mk 14:26–31)
Gethsemane (Mk 14:32–42)
The arrest (Mk 14:43–52)
Jesus before the Sanhedrin (Mk 14:53–65)
Peter's denials (Mk 14:66–72)
Jesus before Pilate (Mk 15:1–15)
Jesus crowned with thorns (Mk 15:16–20)
The way of the cross (Mk 15:21–22)
The crucifixion (Mk 15:23–27)
The crucified Christ is mocked (Mk 15:29–32)
The death of Jesus (Mk 15:33–39)
The holy women of Calvary (Mk 15:40–41)
The burial (Mk 15:42–47)
The empty tomb. The angel's message (Mk 16:1–8)
Appearances of the risen Christ (Mk 16:9–20)[1]

The integrity of this narrative is sound, although many scholars believe that the gospel originally ended at Mk 16:8 and that the final passage of Mk 16:9–20 is a later addition. Some also hold that the first ending has been lost and that the addition of the last section by a copyist was an attempt to rectify the gospel's narrative integrity. Even without the actual accounts of Jesus' appearances in Mk 16:9–20, however, the account represents a tightly knit sequence of events that culminates in the startling news of the Easter proclamation: "Do not be alarmed; you are looking for Jesus of Nazareth, who was crucified. He has been raised; he is not here" (Mk 16:6).

Everything in the passion narrative is oriented toward this simple, joy-filled proclamation of the Easter event. Without this decisive proclamation of the risen Lord, the earlier components of the narrative lose their cohesiveness and unravel from within. The institution narrative of Mark

---

1. These subdivisions are taken from *The Jerusalem Bible* (Garden City, NY: Doubleday, 1966).

14:22–25 is no exception. An examination of its position in the narrative movement of the final three chapters of Mark's gospel shows that it is intimately linked with the events immediately preceding and following it. The events before it depict a mounting sense of the tragedy about to unfold. The anointing at Bethany (Mk 14:3–9) presents Jesus as already aware of his imminent death. The betrayal by Judas (Mk 14:10–11) shows that the plot to have Jesus arrested and put to death (Mk 14:1–2) is already well underway. His decision to celebrate a final Passover meal with his disciples (Mk 14:12–16) sets the stage for his own Passover journey from death to life.

Those events after the meal bring this heightened awareness to its dramatic conclusion. Jesus' agonizing moments at Gethsemane (Mk 14:32–42) give an insight into his struggle to accept his Father's will. His arrest by armed guards (Mk 14:43–52) points to the utter humiliation in store for him. His trial before the Sanhedrin (Mk 14:53–65) depicts the devious means of those wanting him dead. Peter's denials (Mk 14:66–72) show how even those closest to Jesus would abandon him in his time of need. His trial before Pilate (Mk 15:1–15) reveals the deep-seated prejudices of Roman justice. The details of his torture, horrific death, and burial (Mk 15:16–47) uncover the human heart's capacity for brutality and senseless violence.

A Prophetic Action

Of special interest are the two incidents that flank either side of Mark's institution narrative. In the verses immediately preceding it, Jesus foretells his betrayal by Judas: "Truly I tell you, one of you will betray me, one who is eating with me" (Mk 14:18). In the verses immediately after it, he foresees Peter's repeated denial of him before the end of the night: "Truly I tell you, this day, this very night, before the cock crows twice, you will deny me three times" (Mk 14:30). The author of Mark's gospel places the institution narrative between these foreboding predictions of betrayal and denial in order to highlight the deep psychological pain that Jesus will soon undergo. Even as Jesus is breaking bread with his disciples the lonely isolation of his passion has already begun. Jesus is not only going to be betrayed and denied by those closest to him, but he also knows this to be so. The immediate context in which the institution narrative appears depits the Eucharist as being intimately bound up with the circumstances surrounding and flowing from his suffering and death.

By having Jesus foretell Judas' betrayal and Peter's denial, the author of Mark's gospel reveals Jesus' prophetic prowess and presents the institution narrative falling between them in a related light. Jesus' words of blessing on the evening before his death make little sense unless they are understood as a prophetic action representing a New Covenant between God and humanity. The bread and wine that he shares with his disciples symbolize the sacrifice of his body and blood to be given up and poured out for the sake of many. By placing his passion and death in the context of his last Passover meal, Jesus provides his followers with a concrete way of remembrance that exists in continuity with the tradition of their ancestors and that also raises their awareness of a new, definitive action of God in their lives. In this respect, it partakes in those very events that shape his own destiny in the plan of his Father.

In his use of symbolism as a means of communicating the truth of his redemptive mission, Jesus stands in marked continuity with the long tradition of Hebrew prophetic utterance. Hosea's marriage to the faithless Gomer (Hos 1:2–9), Jeremiah's symbols of the loincloth (Jer 13:1–11) and the shattered wine jugs (Jer 13:12–14), Ezekiel's making of bread from a single pot of wheat, barely, beans, lentils, millet, and spelt (Ezek 4:9) and his mime of the emigrant (Ezek 12:1–20) are all examples of the prophetic use of concrete material signs and actions to convey the message of Yahweh to his people. What is so often forgotten when interpreting these actions is that, as authentic utterances of the Word of God, they actually bring into effect what they symbolize: God's word does not return empty (Isa 55:11). In this respect, Jesus' breaking of the bread and drinking of the cup in the company of his disciples brings the event of Calvary into their midst. Before his actual death Jesus makes present the redemptive effects of that first Good Friday in the bread and wine that he eats and drinks with his disciples. These effects culminate in his Easter rising and are already anticipated in his public ministry of teaching and healing.

Mark's Institution Narrative (Mk 14:22–25)

Although it only comprises four verses, the institution narrative itself contains many relevant theological themes. A look at each verse will provide us with some important background for understanding the meaning of the entire account.

1. Verse 22: "While they were eating, he took a loaf of bread, and after blessing it he broke it, gave it to them, and said, 'Take; this is my body.'" Mark introduces us to the institution narrative in the very middle of Jesus' celebration of his Passover meal with his disciples. In doing so, he emphasizes the action about to take place rather than the various incidentals surrounding the meal. This action involves nothing else than the simple blessing and sharing of bread and wine. It is while they were eating that Jesus blesses, breaks, and distributes the "bread of affliction" (Deut 16:3), the unleavened bread that reminds Jews during their traditional Passover celebration of the haste with which their ancestors ate as they set out on their exodus from Egypt. By identifying the bread he is distributing with his body, Jesus gives new meaning to the understanding of the Passover meal. His Last Supper with his disciples is the first Passover of the New Covenant. Rather than leading God's people out of the slavery of Egypt to the Promised Land, he will lead them from the slavery of sin to the fullness of life.

2. Verse 23: "Then he took a cup, and after giving thanks he gave it to them, and all of them drank from it." Scholars agree that this verse probably refers to the third cup of the Passover meal, known as the "cup of benediction." Filled with wine, this cup of blessing normally comes after the main course of lamb and precedes the singing of Psalm 136 or the Great Hallel. This Jewish hymn is recited as an act of thanksgiving for the everlasting kindness of the Lord. Occurring as it does after the eating of the paschal lamb, in this action Jesus draws a connection between himself and the lamb: he is the paschal victim of the New Covenant. He does so not by specifically identifying himself with the lamb that was eaten, but by pointing to the bread and wine that respectively come before and after it. This form of symbolic inclusion strengthens the ties between the Eucharist and what is about to take place on Calvary. The real lamb of sacrifice is the one offered up on the altar of the cross. The bread and wine shared at the Eucharist point to this sacrificial victim and mediate its presence to the believing community.

3. *Verse 24:* "He said to them, 'This is my blood of the covenant, which is poured out for many.'" In this verse Jesus makes it very clear that his actions at the Last Supper are meant to establish a New Covenant between God and his people. Just as he previously identified the unleavened bread of the Passover meal with his body, which would soon be broken on their behalf, he now identifies the cup of wine that he passes to them as his own blood, which will be shed for them and for many others. The specific reference, "the blood of the new covenant," is an allusion to the blood of sacrifice that concluded the covenant of Sinai between God and his people (see Ex 24:8). By alluding to this sacrifice in the context of his last Passover meal Jesus interprets the entire Exodus experience of the Jewish people in a different light. Jesus is not only the new paschal lamb that gives substance to God's people during their new journey from slavery to freedom, but he is also the sacrificial lamb, the death of which will establish a new bond between God and God's people.

4. *Verse 25:* "Truly I tell you, I will never again drink of the fruit of the vine until that day when I drink it new in the kingdom of God." This verse adds an eschatological quality to the institution narrative. As such, it directs the action of Jesus' ritualistic sharing of bread and wine with his disciples toward some future action that will inaugurate God's reign for all time. This action is his upcoming death and burial, the major plot for which has already been set in place (Mk 14:10–11) and for which his body has recently been anointed (Mk 14:3–9). Jesus' reference to drinking the fruit of the vine anew in the kingdom of God refers to the messianic banquet, the definitive sign of the establishment of God's reign. These words give this first Eucharist a peculiar, "already-but-not-yet" quality that has become characteristic of all subsequent celebrations. At the Eucharist, we proclaim, at one and the same time, both the presence of Jesus in our midst and his future coming. The reign of God, for us, is both present and yet to come.

Celebrating Eucharist

This verse-by-verse analysis helps us to understand why Mark presents the institution narrative against the backdrop of the larger narrative of Jesus' passion, death, and resurrection. This decision may seem to have been an obvious choice, since it is generally agreed that Jesus instituted the Eucharist at a supper with his closest disciples the night before he died. It also is generally agreed, however, that the words of the institution narrative stem from a liturgical formula with roots in ancient Palestine, possibly even in Jerusalem itself. By projecting this liturgical pattern back onto the institution narrative itself, and by placing that account within the larger framework of Jesus' passion, death, and resurrection, the author (or the composer of an early passion narrative used by him as a source) consciously intends his audience to find in their common eucharistic worship an authentic encounter with the suffering, dying, and risen Christ.

Mark's institution narrative thus offers sound insights into the prophetic action shared by Jesus with his disciples during his last Passover meal, and this account of the first Eucharist cannot be properly understood apart from the larger, extended narrative about the events relating to Jesus' passion, death, and resurrection. The latter narrative expresses in dramatic form what the former expresses in the symbolic action of sharing bread and passing of a cup of wine. The two, for Mark, are inextricably intertwined.

Mark's institution narrative thus encourages us to view our own celebration of the Eucharist against the backdrop of the larger narrative within which it is cast. Doing so means not only recognizing the intrinsic link that the eucharistic action has with the events of Jesus' passion, death, and resurrection, but also seeing that our lives are intimately bound up with both.

The Eucharist gives each of us the opportunity to discover the mystery of the Christ event reflected in the concrete circumstances of our lives. To gather around the table of the Lord in order to break bread together and to share the cup of blessing is to define our existence entirely in terms of Christ. Not to do so amounts to either a betrayal or, at the very least, a denial of all that Jesus stood for.

Conclusion

Mark writes his gospel to build up our faith. One way he does this is to root the institution narrative in the life of Christ and also in the life of the worshiping community. The two, for him, are closely bound together.

In time the gospels of Matthew and Luke would follow Mark's lead of integrating the account of the institution of the Eucharist into a larger narrative of Jesus' passion, death, and resurrection. Although they would do so to further their own theological aims, they are clearly indebted to Mark for the original way in which he used liturgical texts to reveal the deeper meaning of what occurred during the final hours of Jesus' earthly existence. The lack of an institution narrative in the Gospel of John shows that such an inclusion was not essential to the gospel genre. The decision to include it normally arose from the specific theological goals of the gospel authors themselves.

In the case of Mark's gospel, the inclusion of Jesus' institution of the Eucharist in the Passion narrative is meant to heighten our awareness of our intimate participation in the Christ event. The author of the gospel achieves this aim by introducing a well-known liturgical formula into the institution narrative so that we will have an even deeper sense of the intimate bond between our own celebration of the Eucharist and the events surrounding Jesus' passion, death, and resurrection. In all likelihood, the decision to do so was helped by the conviction that this eucharistic formula represented an authentic tradition in strong continuity with the belief and practice of the earliest Christian community, as well as with the words and teachings of the Lord Jesus himself.

Mark's account of the institution of the Eucharist invites us to become intimately involved in the larger narrative of Jesus' passion, death, and resurrection. From a theological perspective, it reminds us that our celebration of the Eucharist is intimately bound up with the events surrounding Jesus' paschal mystery. Whenever we hear the words of institution—"This is my body…This is my blood"—we are called not only to remember Jesus' passing from life to death, but also to enter into and be shaped by it. Our celebration of the Eucharist reminds us that Jesus' narrative has now become our own. There is no need for us to go back in time. The bread and wine we share give witness to the covenant that binds our stories together, forges our common identity, and forever holds us close.

Reflection Questions

• What in particular strikes you in Mark's account of the institution of the

Eucharist? Does its brevity disappoint you? Does it inspire you? Does it excite your imagination?

• In what way was Jesus' institution of the Eucharist a prophetic action? In what way does it encompass his public ministry? His passion and death? His resurrection?

• What message is Mark trying to convey by incorporating the institution narrative into the larger narrative of Jesus' passion, death, and resurrection? How does this message shape your perception of the Eucharist?

• Do you readily connect the celebration of the Eucharist with the Jesus' passion, death, and resurrection? Do you believe that when participating in the Eucharist you somehow share in that narrative?

Recognizing Jesus

Supper at Emmaus

When he was at the table with them, he took bread, blessed and broke it, and gave it to them. Then their eyes were opened, and they recognized him; and he vanished from their sight. They said to each other, "Were not our hearts burning within us while he was talking to us on the road, while he was opening the scriptures to us?" That same hour they got up and returned to Jerusalem; and they found the eleven and their companions gathered together. (Lk 24:30–33)

I can easily identify with Luke's story of the two disciples on the road to Emmaus (24:13–35). I say this not because I claim to have had any remarkable encounter with the risen Lord, but because many of the sentiments expressed by these disciples correspond to experiences I have had in my own walk of faith. I see them leaving Jerusalem after the troubling events surrounding Jesus' death, and I sense my own distress during times of trial and the accompanying urge I sometimes have to simply walk away from everything. I see them meeting a stranger along the road who gives them new insights into the meaning of their faith, and I sense my own heart burning within me from the deep spiritual wisdom that others have shared with me. I see them sitting together at the table, and I sense the joy of table fellowship that I have experienced among strangers, new acquain-

tances, and cherished friends. I sense their astonishment as they recognize
Jesus' presence in their midst, and I remember those times when I have
sensed the nearness of God in the midst of his seeming absence.

The Christian life has often been described as "a walk with the Lord."
The story of two disciples encountering the Lord on the road to Emmaus
fits this description nicely. Although it leaves much to the imagination, as
one would expect in a narrative aimed at a diverse reading audience, it
gives a strong impression of what such a walk might entail. A close look at
the details of the story bears this out.

1. Departure from Jerusalem (vv. 13–14)

The account begins with two disciples leaving Jerusalem on the very day
of Jesus' resurrection (v. 13). It is not clear why they have chosen to leave
the holy city just a few days after Jesus' death and at a time when stories
were already circulating about the empty tomb and of Jesus still being
alive. Perhaps they had some business to attend to at this small village just
seven miles away from Jerusalem. Perhaps they were overwhelmed by
what was happening and needed to put some distance between themselves
and the others who had followed Jesus from Galilee to Judea. Perhaps they
were despondent over his death and were leaving the city out of disillu-
sionment and the sudden loss of their deepest hopes. Perhaps they were
afraid for their lives and were fleeing the city (and the authorities) to
remove themselves from danger and to disassociate themselves from
recent events. Perhaps their motivations were mixed, and they were leaving for a variety of reasons, conscious and unconscious.

Whatever their motives, these two disciples, Cleopas and another whose
identity remains hidden (possibly his wife?), are talking about all that had
happened in the past few days (v. 14) and seem to be overwhelmed by a
deep sense of sadness. This pall of sadness is understandable, given the
recent loss of their Master and the newly surfaced questions about the disappearance of his body. As they leave Jerusalem they do not know what to
believe. They are reflecting on their experience, however, as they make
their way to Emmaus (v. 14). Perhaps they are trying to discern what their
next move should be.

2. The Appearance of Jesus (vv. 15–24)

While they are discussing what had happened over the past few days, Jesus comes to them and accompanies them on their way (v. 15). Their failure to recognize him (v. 16) indicates that something has changed, either in Jesus himself or in their perception of him. As they make their way to Emmaus, Jesus engages them by inquiring about the topic of their conversation (v. 17). This seemingly innocent question stops the two disciples dead in their tracks. They cannot believe that anyone could be unacquainted with the recent events that had taken place in Jerusalem. Nor do they understand how anyone could possibly be involved in discussing anything else (v. 18).

Their surprise is indicative of their past and reveals their own inner turmoil. Prior to their coming to Jerusalem, the world of the two disciples had centered fully on their Master. Without him to fall back on, they are uneasy about their present situation and confused about what the future would bring. Jesus' question allows them to take stock of their situation. Cleopas and his companion recount the circumstances surrounding Jesus' condemnation and death. They also mention the disconcerting news concerning the disappearance of his body, the women's story of a vision of angels, and the news that he might still be alive. Their hope that Jesus was the one to redeem Israel has dwindled to a mere flicker, if even that (vv. 19–24).

The reader gets a strong sense that, in leaving Jerusalem, Cleopas and his companion wish to put the events of the past few days behind them. Going to Emmaus was to be the first step of a long process of distancing themselves from their shattered lives and then picking up the pieces.

Much to their surprise, however, the process never fully gets underway. Jesus has something else in mind and has already begun doing something about it: he approaches the two disciples; he initiates the conversation; he spends time listening to what they have to say. Only after they have been given the opportunity to reflect upon their experiences and tell their story does Jesus attempt a response.

3. The Teaching of Jesus (vv. 25–27)

He begins with what seems like a reprimand: "Oh, how foolish you are, and how slow of heart to believe all that the prophets have declared! Was it not necessary that the Messiah should suffer these things and then enter into his glory?"(v. 25). Jesus' intention is not obvious from the literal meaning of the words. One can easily imagine him using the tone and inflection of his voice to convey a sense that would be more akin to sad disappointment or an unsettling disquiet than the sharp criticism that his words are normally taken for. It also seems unlikely that someone like Jesus would spend time gaining the trust of his companions by listening to their experience of the last few days only to distance himself from them by criticizing them for their inability to see the hand of God in the recent events. We need to see Jesus saying these words in a way that would invite his companions to listen to his words with their hearts. Only then will his explanation of the Scriptures make sense to them. Only then will he be able to open up Moses and the prophets in a way that will keep his companions' interest and make their hearts burn within them (vv. 26–27).

The reader gets the sense that Jesus both catches his companions' attention and goes on talking to them for quite some time. One also senses that his companions are eager listeners. Perhaps it was because they had felt listened to and understood by Jesus that they were able to reciprocate so easily. Perhaps it was the deep spiritual bond between them that, despite their inability to recognize him, led them to find in his interpretation of the Scriptures a new way of understanding their own experiences. Perhaps, too, it was his casual way of approaching them and of asking the right question that helped them to see what was truly important in their lives and what was of only secondary value.

In any case, one can imagine the time passing very quickly as the two disciples make their way with Jesus toward their destination. As they approach Emmaus, one wonders if they have pondered the identity of the stranger who had befriended them upon the way. Who is this man who is unraveling the meaning of the Scriptures before their eyes? How does he know so much about what Moses and the prophets had foretold about the Messiah? And how does he know that it all pertains to Jesus of Nazareth, the one whom the chief priest and leaders had just delivered up to death? One wonders if, even now, the disciples are beginning to see on the stranger's face some faint marks of recognition, if what was previously unknown is now slowly coming to light.

4. The Breaking of the Bread (vv. 28–31)

When they near the village Jesus is about to take his leave of his companions and continue his journey (v. 28). He does not wish to overstay his welcome. He does not force himself on anyone. If he is not invited to stay, he will simply go on his way. He will remain with them only if they ask him. His companions on the road choose to do so.

It is growing dark, and the two disciples press him to stay with them (v. 29). Perhaps they hope he will continue to teach them and make the words of Scripture come alive for them. Perhaps they feel sorry for him, a stranger traveling all alone on a dark country road. Perhaps they wish to offer him hospitality, a hot meal, and a warm bed before he continues his journey the next day. Jesus agrees and goes in to eat and presumably to take lodging with them.

While they are at supper, he takes the bread, pronounces the blessing, breaks it, and begins to distribute it to them (v. 30). At that moment, something happens. Time seems to stand still. A dark veil is lifted from their eyes, and the disciples suddenly recognize the man before them as Jesus, their Master (v. 31).

Unfortunately, they have little, if any, time to react. Before they can think or say or do anything, their companion vanishes from their sight and is nowhere to be found (v. 31). Jesus has come to them, revealed himself to them, and quickly taken his leave of them. He has been present to his disciples in a way they had never before experienced. He has disappeared, but they still feel as though he is very close to them. The broken bread on the plate before them reminds them of what he had said to his disciples just a few nights before: "This is my body, which is given for you. Do this in remembrance of me" (Lk 22:19). They also remember how their hearts burned within them when he was explaining the Scriptures to them along the road (v. 32). How could they not have recognized him then? What was it that kept them from seeing him in their strange traveling companion? They are suddenly filled with a sense of urgency and purpose (v. 33). Everything in their lives has come together—and they remember that it all took place during the breaking of the bread.

5. Return to Jerusalem (vv. 33–35)

The disciples cannot contain their excitement over what they have just experienced. They cannot finish their meal and, even though the day is far spent, they do not wish to spend the night at Emmaus and wait until morning before deciding their next move (v. 33a). More important, they seem to have no doubts or second thoughts about what they have just experienced. Jesus, their Master, the one who was to redeem Israel, is alive; they had experienced him in the breaking of the bread. Their momentary recognition of him has changed their entire outlook on their situation. Their sadness has lifted. Their need to distance themselves from the events of the preceding days has itself vanished. Their need to be at Emmaus has likewise faded to the background. At this moment in their lives, the only thing they need to do is to tell the others, those back in Jerusalem. Nothing else is more urgent. They need only to spread the news—and as quickly as possible.

Without another thought, they leave their meal and set out for the holy city to tell their fellow disciples that they have seen the risen Lord (v. 33a). The impact of their experience turns them around and sends them back to the scattered group of disciples they have left behind. They recognize their experience as a communal treasure that needs to be shared with the other followers of Jesus. Little do they know the consequences of their decision to go back and confront the situation they have left behind. Their lives would never be the same. From their experience—and that of others—the first Christian community would gradually take shape.

They set out toward Jerusalem and, much to their surprise, they find upon their arrival the Eleven and the rest of the company assembled together (v. 33b). Before a word can leave their lips, they themselves are greeted with the Good News: "The Lord has risen indeed, and he has appeared to Simon!" (v. 34). Jesus has not wasted any time. He has gone before them and prepared the way.

The event at Emmaus was not unique. Others had experienced him as well. Confirmed in the validity of their experience, the disciples' recount their experience of the stranger they had met along the road (v. 35). The understanding of the Christ event was slowly taking shape in the lives of the early disciples. From then on, their celebration of Eucharist, the breaking of the bread, would be central to their lives and a constituent element of Christ's body. It could be no other way.

The Story's Relevance

The story of the disciples on their way to Emmaus plays a pivotal role in Luke's account of Jesus' post-resurrectional appearances. It does so for a number of reasons.

1. For one thing, it shows Jesus appearing not to those in Jesus' inner circle (e.g., to the Eleven or to close friends of Jesus like Martha and Mary), but to two ordinary disciples with no other claim to prominence. Were it not for this single gospel pericope, these two disciples would have remained completely unknown to us. As it stands, other than the name Cleopas (the other disciple remains completely anonymous) we know virtually nothing about their lives and situation in life. This biblical anonymity touches us in an important way. In many ways, we too are anonymous witnesses to Christ. The story reaffirms our belief that Jesus has come not for a select few, but for all who seek God with a sincere heart.

2. It also reminds us that Jesus sometimes comes to us when we least expect it and are poorly inclined to recognize him. In the Emmaus story, he joins his disciples during an in-between time, while they are on the road, traveling from one place to another. They do not plan his coming; nor could they even think of doing so. He simply walks up to them and engages them in conversation. What is more, they do not recognize him until they reach their destination for the night and gather around the table to share the evening meal. Jesus approaches us in a similar way. Our God is a God of surprises. He comes to us in many ways and at various times and circumstances. For this reason we need to expect the unexpected and hope that we are able to recognize him when the right moment arrives.

3. The story, moreover, bolsters our attachment to the Eucharist as the center of Christian life and practice. The disciples at Emmaus recognize Jesus during the breaking of the bread. The eucharistic overtones of this passage invite us to examine our own understanding of what takes place during the eucharistic celebration. During this sacred liturgical action, Christ comes to us in a special way, making himself present to us through the Scriptures, in the breaking of the bread, in the worshiping community, and in the person

of the presiding priest. The popularity of the story is directly related to the Christian community's understanding that the eucharistic celebration is central to its life. During it, we too are given a glimpse of the risen Christ and confirm our faith in his presence in our midst.

4. Finally, the story provides us with a good indication of what the walk of discipleship entails: (1) The disciples set out toward Emmaus reflecting on their experience of Christ's passion and death. (2) The risen Lord accompanies them on their way unrecognized, engages them in conversation, questions them, and allows them to share their understanding of the events that had recently shaped their lives. (3) After listening to them, he opens up the Scriptures to them, showing them how Moses and the prophets foretold what the Messiah had to undergo in order to enter into glory. (4) He accepts their invitation to sup with them and reveals himself to them in the breaking of the bread. (5) This experience changes their lives and sends them back to share the Good News with those they had left behind in Jerusalem. Self-reflection. Listening. Teaching. Eucharist. Proclamation. These are the experiences that the disciples encounter on their journey. They are the same experiences that help to shape us as disciples of Christ today.

To summarize: Following Christ means reflecting on our experience of Christ's presence in our lives, articulating that experience, and listening to it. It also involves finding a reflection of that experience in the Scriptures and validating it with Christ in the breaking of the bread. Finally, it means sharing with others what we have come to recognize about ourselves and Christ in the process. All of this takes place in the context of a journey with Christ where he remains largely unrecognized, except through the eyes of faith. During that journey, the Eucharist is a sacred resting place where we glimpse the Lord's presence in our lives and become empowered to face our responsibilities with renewed vigor. It also is the place where we renew our commitment to be members of Christ's body and learn to live life with a sense of immediacy and urgency. This process of self-reflection, listening, teaching, Eucharist, and proclamation composes the fundamental rhythm of the life of discipleship, one that can carry us through even the most difficult of times. The experience of the two disciples on the road to Emmaus bears this out. Their experience on the very day (v. 13) of Christ's resurrection has become a metaphor for the journey of faith and the great joy that comes from recognizing Jesus in the breaking of the bread.

Conclusion

We are all on the road to Emmaus. Like the two disciples in Luke's account, we are called to travel that road twice: away from Jerusalem and back again. During our journey we are called to integrate our difficulties with the faith through self-reflection, listening, the study of Scripture, breaking bread together, and sharing. Engaging in this daily practice of discipleship effects a change in us. Even if we find ourselves at the end of the day in the same physical place, our walk of faith gently brings us to a different place in our relationship with God.

Jesus accompanies us on this walk. He seeks us out, questions us, listens to us, teaches us, and has fellowship with us. Unfortunately, much of this occurs without our full awareness of what is happening. He seems a stranger to us, and we often fail to recognize him. Even when we do, he quickly vanishes from sight, leaving us with nothing but burning hearts and a deep desire to share with others the knowledge of his deep love for us. Jesus leaves us, but never abandons us. Wherever we journey, he is never very far away. We are reminded of this whenever we open the Scriptures, break bread together, or encounter a stranger in our midst.

The story of the two disciples on the road to Emmaus is our story. It tells us that we who are anonymous in the eyes of the world are known and loved by God. It reminds us of the centrality of the Eucharist for our daily walk of faith. It depicts the life of discipleship as a process of growth that enables us to embrace community and to contribute to its well being. It lets us know that Christ sometimes comes to us when we least expect it, during those in-between times when we are on the way, in the middle of a journey, when our bodies (and perhaps even our spirits) are tired and our eyes too weary to see.

Reflection Questions

• Have you ever found yourself disheartened and disillusioned like the disciples on the road to Emmaus? If so, how did you deal with those difficult times? Did anyone walk beside you and encourage you? How did the experience weaken or deepen your faith? Where was Jesus during this time of confusion? Absent from your life? Beside you? Leading you?

• Have you ever felt as though you have encountered Jesus in the Scriptures or while in the presence of others? If so, what was the experience like? If not, would you like to have such an experience?

• What does it mean to be a disciple of Jesus? Do you consider yourself one? Do others consider you one?

• What does it mean to recognize Jesus in the breaking of the bread?

• Do you consider yourself a part of Jesus' inner circle or an anonymous follower on the periphery? Does Jesus walk with you in your journey through life? Do you share that experience with others?

Eucharistic Faith

The Bread of Life

So they said to him, "What sign are you going to give us then, so that we may see it and believe you? What work are you performing? Our ancestors ate the manna in the wilderness; as it is written, 'He gave them bread from heaven to eat.'" Then Jesus said to them, "Very truly, I tell you, it was not Moses who gave you the bread from heaven, but it is my Father who gives you the true bread from heaven. For the bread of God is that which comes down from heaven and gives life to the world." (Jn 6:30–33)

Where would we be without signs? Hopelessly lost, I would imagine. It would be like trying to go through life with our eyes closed. Try doing so for a few minutes and you will learn that it is not an easy task by anyone's standards. Signs are a very important part of human existence. We need them to point us in the right direction, to give us assurance that we are on the right path, and to help us mark the various destinations and goals we set for ourselves. We communicate with each other through signs. Human language is nothing but a complex system of signs and symbols that enables us to express our thoughts and feelings to one another. Without signs we would be hopelessly out of touch with each other. We would be unable to interact with our environment in any kind of sustained, meaningful way. We would also be unable to communicate with God.

The Eucharist is a sign given to us by God to affirm God's deep love for us and his presence in our midst. Because it is given to us by God, however, it does not merely point something out to us, but actually puts us in touch with the mystery it seeks to reveal. In his "Discourse on the Bread of Life" (Jn 6:22–71), Jesus affirms himself as the "Bread of Life" (Jn 6:35). He tells us that his flesh and blood are real food and drink (Jn 6:55). He offers eternal life to anyone who receives them (Jn 6:58).

It is impossible to remain neutral to such claims. We must either accept or reject them. There is no middle ground. The author of John's gospel uses this sacramental realism to highlight the continuity between the earthly Jesus, the resurrected Christ, and the Lord's presence in the Eucharist. So strong is this emphasis that he often allows the historical Jesus to speak as though he has already passed into his exalted, glorified state. To this end, Jesus' discourse conveys strong eucharistic overtones and underscores the importance of faith in Jesus for those wishing to enter eternal life. He identifies himself as "the living bread that came down from heaven" (Jn 6:51). Unlike the sign given to the Jews during their desert sojourn, this bread gives life to the world and the promise of eternity to all who receive it.

The Book of Signs

Scholars generally divide the Gospel of John into two parts: "The Book of Signs" (Jn 1:19—12:50) and "The Book of Glory" (Jn: 13:1—20:31). Jesus' "Discourse on the Bread of Life" is part of "The Book of Signs."

The evangelist's primary aim in "The Book of Signs" is to depict the Word of God revealing himself to the world through a series of concrete signs or manifestations of divine power. There are seven in all: (1) the changing of water into wine at the wedding at Cana (Jn 2:1–12), (2) the cure of the nobleman's son (Jn 4:43–54), (3) the cure of the sick man at the Pool of Bethesda (Jn 5:1–15), (4) the multiplication of the loaves and fish (Jn 6:1–15), (5) Jesus walking on water (Jn 6:16–21), (6) the cure of the man born blind (Jn 9:1–40), and (7) the raising of Lazarus from the dead (Jn 11:1–44).

These signs are more than miracles, in the traditional sense of a divine intervention in human affairs, because they reveal something about the identity of Jesus. Through them the evangelist depicts Jesus as the fullness of God's revelation to humanity. The carpenter of Nazareth manifests, for John, the very nature of God. Jesus is the Word of God dwelling among us who commands the elements, makes decisions over life and death, and holds the key to eternal life.

Appearing in chapter six of John's gospel, the "Discourse on the Bread of Life" has close ties to the fourth and fifth signs. One might go so far as to say that it reveals their true meaning, or, in the very least, that they set the stage for one of the most startling assertions that Jesus would make regarding his mission and personal identity. The eucharistic overtones of the fourth sign (i.e., the multiplication of the loaves and fishes [Jn 6:1–15]) and the suspension of nature's rules in the fifth (i.e., Jesus walking on water [Jn 6:16–21]) anticipate the teaching of the discourse and point to the fundamental choice that Jesus will ultimately ask of his listeners—whether or not to believe in his divinity. John's gospel was written for the primary purpose of convincing its readers of the truth of Jesus' divinity. Jesus' eucharistic discourse contributes to this goal and directs the dramatic movement of the narrative to its ultimate conclusion in "The Book of Glory."

An Engaging Conversation

The discourse itself can be likened to an extended dialogue between Jesus and those who followed his trail of signs and miracles throughout the countryside of ancient Palestine. Its setting takes place in Galilee with the crowd looking for Jesus near the city of Tiberias on the shore of the lake. After some initial setbacks, they finally catch up with him on the other side where he is giving instruction at a synagogue in the fishing village of Capernaum (see Jn 6:59). The dialogue begins thus:

> When they found him on the other side of the sea, they said to him, "Rabbi, when did you come here?" Jesus answered them, "Very truly, I tell you, you are looking for me, not because you saw signs, but because you ate your fill of the loaves. Do not work for the food that perishes, but for the food that endures for eternal life, which the Son of Man will give you. For it is on him that God the Father has set his seal." Then they said to him, "What must we do to perform the works

of God?" Jesus answered them, "This is the work of God, that you believe in him whom he has sent." (Jn 6:25–29)

Given the great difficulty they had in finding him, the crowd's opening question is most appropriate and not at all unusual. If Jesus did not set out with his disciples in the only boat along the shore (Jn 6:22), how could he have made his way to the other side of the lake so quickly? Jesus responds to this seemingly innocuous question by confronting his hearers with their real motives for following him. He warns them that they should be doing so not for material benefit, but to gain eternal life. When asked what such a work might specifically entail, he tells them that they must have faith in him. Here, Jesus brings to the fore the necessity of faith for anyone who wishes to be his follower. To believe in Jesus as the One sent by God (Jn 6:29) is not merely peripheral to the gospel message, but one of its central, identifying marks. Unless one places one's faith in Jesus, the Son of Man on whom "God the Father has set his seal" (Jn 6:27), one cannot work for "the food that endures for eternal life" (Jn 6:27). Indeed, one can "perform" this work of God (Jn 6:29) only by receiving it. Jesus gives it, however, only to those who place their faith in him.

As the conversation continues, the crowd asks Jesus for some evidence to back up his dramatic request for faith:

So they said to him, "What sign are you going to give us then, so that we may see it and believe you? What work are you performing? Our ancestors ate the manna in the wilderness; as it is written, 'He gave them bread from heaven to eat.'" Then Jesus said to them, "Very truly, I tell you, it was not Moses who gave you the bread from heaven, but it is my Father who gives you the true bread from heaven. For the bread of God is that which comes down from heaven and gives life to the world." (Jn 6:30–33)

Once again, the question posed to Jesus by the crowd is not at all unusual, especially in an atmosphere that has the Old Testament for its experiential backdrop, and most especially in the context of a synagogue instruction. The history of Israel is marked with dramatic signs given by God to his people for the express purpose of leading them out of slavery to freedom. By asking Jesus for a sign so that they can put their faith in him, the people are merely following the example of their ancestors, who asked for and received manna from heaven to sustain them during their desert sojourn.

In his response Jesus reminds his listeners that God, not Moses, gave their ancestors this "bread from heaven" (Jn 6:31) and that his Father in heaven will give them "the true bread from heaven" (Jn 6:32), the kind that will give life to the world. Here Jesus emphasizes the divine quality of the sign given the Israelites during their wanderings in the desert. He then extends the analogy to the situation of his hearers by telling them that his Father in heaven will supply them with the bread of everlasting life (Jn 6:32). By claiming that Moses did not give the Israelites manna from heaven (Jn 6:32), but that he and his Father in heaven would give them the food of eternal life (Jn 6:27, 32), Jesus highlights his intimate relationship with the Father. In doing so, he calls attention (at least implicitly) to his glorified, divine status. This claim will become even more explicit as the conversation continues.

The next part of the discourse reveals the first sign of discord between Jesus and his listeners. The crowd enjoins Jesus to give them the bread of which he has spoken:

> They said to him, "Sir, give us this bread always." Jesus said to them, "I am the bread of life. Whoever comes to me will never be hungry, and whoever believes in me will never be thirsty. But I said to you that you have seen me and yet do not believe. Everything that the Father gives me will come to me, and anyone who comes to me I will never drive away; for I have come down from heaven, not to do my own will, but the will of him who sent me. And this is the will of him who sent me, that I should lose nothing of all that he has given me, but raise it up on the last day. This is indeed the will of my Father, that all who see the Son and believe in him may have eternal life; and I will raise them up on the last day." Then the Jews began to complain about him because he said, "I am the bread that came down from heaven." They were saying, "Is not this Jesus, the son of Joseph, whose father and mother we know? How can he now say, 'I have come down from heaven'?" (Jn 6:34–42)

The crowd murmurs in protest because Jesus claims to be the bread from heaven that gives not only life to the world, but eternal life itself. The people can accept him as a prophet and great miracle worker, but they cannot bring themselves to believe that he can give them eternal life. After all, they know his parents and where he comes from (Jn 6:42). How could someone from such a background provide them with such heavenly treasure? Jesus' hearers cannot accept even the possibility that he could carry out such a promise. Furthermore, by identifying himself as the bread of life, he also brings them face to face with the extremely distasteful, even disgusting, prospect of eating human flesh. The Jews, in particular, would quickly back away from even the slightest hint of paganism, a prospect that surely would have entered their minds by the passage's underlying implication of ritualistic cannibalism.

Jesus responds to the crowd's protestations with a further assertion of his extraordinary claims:

> Jesus answered them, "Do not complain among yourselves. No one can come to me unless drawn by the Father who sent me; and I will raise that person up on the last day. It is written in the prophets, 'And they shall all be taught by God.' Everyone who has heard and learned from the Father comes to me. Not that anyone has seen the Father except the one who is from God; he has seen the Father. Very truly, I tell you, whoever believes has eternal life. I am the bread of life. Your ancestors ate the manna in the wilderness, and they died. This is the bread that comes down from heaven, so that one may eat of it and not die. I am the living bread that came down from heaven. Whoever eats of this bread will live forever; and the bread that I will give for the life of the world is my flesh." (Jn 6:43–51)

Here, Jesus' divinity receives its strongest statement yet. He claims not only to have come from the Father, but also to be the only one who has seen him. The Father sent him to the world as the living bread that will give life to the world. He presents this revelation as a teaching of God (Jn 6:45). Only those who believe in Jesus and who eat his flesh will receive eternal life. Jesus himself will raise them up on the last day.

One can certainly understand the apprehensions of those present in the synagogue. Jesus claims an intimacy with the Father that gives him a divine or, at the very least, a semi-divine status. He places himself above Moses and claims to have the power to raise people up on the last day.

More than that, he asserts that he himself is the very food that will give people eternal life. All that is required is for people to believe in him and to feed on his flesh.

Jesus has not backtracked at all from those murmuring against him. With his hearers now arguing among themselves, he becomes even more explicit in his teaching:

> The Jews then disputed among themselves, saying, "How can this man give us his flesh to eat?" So Jesus said to them, "Very truly, I tell you, unless you eat the flesh of the Son of Man and drink his blood, you have no life in you. Those who eat my flesh and drink my blood have eternal life, and I will raise them up on the last day; for my flesh is true food and my blood is true drink. Those who eat my flesh and drink my blood abide in me, and I in them. Just as the living Father sent me, and I live because of the Father, so whoever eats me will live because of me. This is the bread that came down from heaven, not like that which your ancestors ate, and they died. But the one who eats this bread will live forever." (Jn 6:52–58)

Jesus' teaching culminates in this final section of the discourse. He presents his hearers with a teaching from God that runs against all the major currents of the official Judaism of his day. He depicts himself as someone greater than Moses, with a divine nature, an intimate, exclusive knowledge of the Father, and the means of bestowing eternal life. He offers nourishment to his hearers through the teaching he imparts and through his body and blood, which he identifies as "the bread of life." Only those who believe in him and his teaching and who eat his body and blood will be raised up on the last day. Only they will receive life and live it fully for all eternity.

Jesus presents his hearers with difficult words. Never before had anyone spoken this way, and no one would ever do so again. His teaching represents a decisive turn in the history of salvation. It would be impossible to remain indifferent to it. One must either accept or reject it. There is no middle ground.

The Reaction

Jesus' discourse produces mixed reactions among his hearers. The majority of those present continue their murmuring: "This teaching is difficult;

who can accept it?" (Jn 6:60). This number includes not only those members of the crowd who followed Jesus around for strictly material interests and related concerns, but even some of his disciples.

With the "Discourse on the Bread of Life," Jesus moves teaching about himself and his mission on earth to a higher plane. Many who had been attracted to his words become discouraged and turn away. Aware that even some of his disciples are murmuring against him, he challenges them with the call to faith:

> "Does this offend you? Then what if you were to see the Son of Man ascending to where he was before? It is the spirit that gives life; the flesh is useless. The words that I have spoken to you are spirit and life. But among you there are some who do not believe." For Jesus knew from the first who were the ones that did not believe, and who was the one that would betray him. And he said, "For this reason I have told you that no one can come to me unless it is granted by the Father." (Jn 6:61–65)

Even these words do not stop some of Jesus' disciples from leaving him. They refuse to remain with him any longer. One gets the impression that only the Twelve stick by him. When he turns to them and asks them if they too wish to leave, Simon Peter replies, "Lord, to whom can we go? You have the words of eternal life. We have come to believe and know that you are the Holy One of God" (Jn 6:68–69).

This profession of faith is what Jesus has been seeking all along from his listeners. It should surprise no one that he elicits it from those closest to him, that intimate circle of followers he called "the Twelve." This profession of faith is particularly important because, unlike other gospel narratives, John's does not contain any specific account of the call of the apostles. This omission might possibly be explained by the firm conviction on the part of the author that such a call was intimately connected to the response of faith. That response confirms the vocation of the Twelve, binds them even more closely to their master, and is intimately tied to what they have handed on to the Christian community.

As stated earlier, the author of John's gospel often allows the earthly Jesus to speak as though he is already in glory. By binding Jesus' pre- and post-resurrectional existences so closely together, he produces a narrative that strongly supports Jesus' divine status. What is more, Jesus' "Discourse on the Bread of Life" gives the author the opportunity to make this claim in a liturgical setting. We have already seen that the discourse takes place when Jesus is teaching at a synagogue in Capernaum (Jn 6:59). Through this setting of Sabbath worship, the evangelist gives his readers the subtle indication that Jesus' teaching on the bread of life can best be understood in the context of their own form of communal worship, the Eucharist. In such a setting Jesus' words on the living bread take on deeper significance.

Hearing this discourse in the context of a eucharistic celebration heightens the hearers' awareness of the true meaning of what is about to take place. At the Eucharist Christians are nourished both by the teaching of God (Jn 6:45) and by Jesus' own body and blood (Jn 6:51–58). Each time it is celebrated, Christians are confronted with the call to faith. The response of faith cannot be presumed. Even today there are so-called disciples of Jesus who do not take his teaching seriously and who have distanced themselves radically from him in their hearts. At the same time, many others have accepted the challenge of faith and confirmed the true depth of their commitment to him.

Conclusion

Jesus' "Discourse on the Bread of Life" reminds us of the centrality of faith to the gospel message. It affirms the continuity between the earthly and risen Lord and demonstrates this fundamental tenet of the faith by allowing the Jesus of glory to speak through an instruction given by Jesus in a synagogue at Capernaum during his public ministry. The liturgical setting of this instruction would have led the early Christian community to interpret the discourse in terms of their eucharistic worship. The same holds true for us today.

During the church's eucharistic worship, Jesus comes to us as the bread that gives life to the world. To participate in the Eucharist requires the faith of the Twelve, a heartfelt belief that Jesus is God's holy one who possesses the words of eternal life. For the true disciple there is nowhere else to go. The discourse presents us with a fundamental and radical choice: to embrace Jesus' words or to reject them. Those who accept them will never thirst or go hungry again.

Jesus offers us nourishment of both Word and sacrament. The eucharistic celebration brings these two forms of nourishment to the people of God. Jesus is the living Word and the bread come down from heaven. Those who listen to him and feed on his body and blood will live in him and receive life to the full. The Eucharist is the seal of that promise. It opens our eyes and points us toward God. It is a living sign of God's presence in our midst, an action of Christ, "the work of God" par excellence. Those who participate in it remain in Jesus and he in them. His words become their words. The love they share binds them closely to each other—and endures forever.

Reflection Questions

• What meaning do you find in Jesus' "Discourse on the Bread of Life"? What statements do you accept? Are there any you find hard to accept or perhaps might even reject?

• Does a part of you murmur against Jesus' claims? Do any of his claims stretch the limits of credibility? Does a part of you seek a sign that will prove the truth of his claims? Can you do without such signs?

• Do you believe, with Peter, that Jesus has the words of eternal life? If so, what has brought you to such an affirmation? If not, would you like to believe?

• Do you believe that Jesus is the Bread of Life? What does it mean to eat the flesh of the Son of Man and to drink his blood? What does this saying have to do with the Eucharist? What does it have to do with Jesus' passion, death, and resurrection?

A Call to Service

Washing the Disciples' Feet

Jesus, knowing that the Father had given all things into his hands, and that he had come from God and was going to God, got up from the table, took off his outer robe, and tied a towel around himself. Then he poured water into a basin and began to wash the disciples' feet and to wipe them with the towel that was tied around him. (Jn 13:3–5)

In Jesus' day, washing somebody's feet was the work of a servant. It was one of the most menial tasks anyone could perform. This was especially true in ancient Palestine, where residue from the dusty roads and hot desert air would cake to one's skin and the leather of one's sandals.

For the Jews, washing the feet of one's guests was an expression of hospitality. It refreshed the visitor and made him or her feel welcome. It was also practical and hygienic, for it helped to keep one's home relatively free of unwanted dust and sand. In wealthy homes servants were typically assigned this ordinary, mundane task. In more modest households it was looked after by one of the women or even the children. In all cases, it was considered a tedious but necessary chore that was extended to everyone who crossed one's threshold, especially those who were invited to a meal.

When was the last time you washed somebody's feet? Probably not in a long while, I would venture to say. Although we have found other ways of keeping our homes clean and extending hospitality to guests, this simple gesture continues to epitomize the meaning of humble service.

It is not by accident that the part of John's gospel known as "The Book of Glory" begins with the account of Jesus washing the feet of his disciples (Jn 13:1–20). During the Last Supper, which the evangelist tells us took place sometime before the feast of the Passover (v. 1), Jesus performs this highly symbolic gesture in order to impress upon his closest disciples his fundamental reason for coming into the world and leaving it. This prophetic action effects what it signifies. It reminds us that everything in Jesus' life must be understood in the context of humble service—even the institution of the Eucharist. It also highlights the essential characteristic par excellence of Christian discipleship. To be a follower of Jesus means to walk in his footsteps and to dedicate ourselves to the welfare of others. In the place of an institution narrative, the author of John's gospel gives us a concrete example of the direction our following of Christ should take.

Narrative and Community

To understand the significance of Jesus washing the feet of his disciples, it is first necessary to view it in the context of the larger narrative, of which it represents but a small (albeit very significant) part. The Gospel of John underwent a long process of composition roughly between the years 50-120 A.D. In its final form, as we have noted, it seeks to demonstrate Jesus' divine sonship by weaving in, throughout the narrative, sayings from Jesus in his glorified state. The liturgical assembly for which it was intended would have had little difficulty in accepting the continuity of the historical and the glorified Jesus. It was their firm belief that the Jesus who walked the shores of the Sea of Galilee just a few generations earlier was the very same person who was glorified by God through his passion, death, and resurrection, and who entered their midst during their weekly celebration of the Eucharist.

One reason why the gospel does not contain Jesus' actual words of institution over the bread and wine may be because these phrases had already been thoroughly integrated into the ritual action of the local believing community for which it was intended. Perhaps the gospel writer thought that by omitting them from the texts the community listened to during the Liturgy of the Word, they would take on even greater meaning when heard during the Liturgy of the Eucharist. In such an instance, the liturgical background of the gospel offers valuable insights into its organization and possible purpose as an inspired text.

As we have already noted, scholars divide the Gospel of John into two parts: "The Book of Signs" (Jn 1:19—12:50) and "The Book of Glory" (Jn 13:1—20:31). This diptych structure is filled out by an opening Prologue (Jn 1:1–18) and an epilogue that deals with Galilean resurrection appearances and serves as a second conclusion (Jn 21:1–25). Scholars generally agree that "The Book of Signs" explains the meaning of Jn 1:11 ("He came to what was his own, and his own people did not accept him "). "The Book of Glory," in turn, develops the meaning of Jn 1:12 ("But to all who received him, who believed in his name, he gave power to become children of God").

These two parts set the person of Jesus in his glorified state before the believing community and remind it of how he was rejected by his own and of how those who believe in him have become God's adopted children. By pondering these stories believers are led to encounter the depth of their own belief in the power of the glorified Lord to work powerful signs in their midst and to effectively make them sons and daughters of God. All of this, of course, is done in the context of the liturgical assembly, where "sign" and "glory" merge in the ritual action of the breaking of the bread and the passing of the cup. In Jesus, who is the "Bread of Life" (Jn 6: 35), bread and wine both signify and impart the glory of eternal life to those who believe in him.

A Eucharistic Action

Coming as it does at the very beginning of "The Book of Glory," the account of Jesus washing the feet of his disciples encapsulates many of the evangelist's most significant themes. At the same time, its striking symbolic action serves as a bridge between the various signs given by Jesus during the gospel's first major section and the process of exaltation that takes place by virtue of Jesus' passion, death, and resurrection. For these reasons, it is entirely fitting that John's account of the Last Supper should serve as the hinge upon which the diptych structure of the gospel swings.

The Eucharist in John's gospel is depicted as "the sign" par excellence given by Jesus to the community of believers. It effectively embraces all that he would undergo for humanity in his paschal mystery. The central place given to the washing of the feet in this account underscores in a vivid way the drama that is about to take place in Jesus' life and, through him, in the lives of all who believe in him. Jesus performs this action fully cognizant of the significance of the meal he is celebrating with his closest disciples and well aware that one of them is about to betray him (v. 2). Once he performs this action, moreover, he goes out of his way to impress upon his listeners the significance of what they have just experienced (vv. 12–20).

In the washing of the disciples' feet, word and symbol come together in a powerful, truly prophetic way. One might go so far as to say that the significance of this humble expression permeates all that is then taking place (in the Last Supper), that is about to take place (in Jesus' passion, death, and resurrection), and that will take place (in the life of the Christian community). The multilayered significance of this action parallels what is taking place in the eucharistic mystery itself. Jesus' exaltation, in other words, is preceded by his divine humiliation. Just as he had come from and was bound to return to God (v. 3), Jesus enters the world of each eucharistic assembly, becoming for them their very food and drink, so that he might take them to the Father and be an instrument of their divinization.

A Call to Service

A close look at the various components of Jesus' symbolic washing reveals the nature of the drama that it embodies. Seven points in particular come to the fore.

1. During Supper (v. 2). To begin with, the washing takes place during the celebration of the Last Supper. During this time, the powers of darkness have already infiltrated Jesus' inner circle. In the person of Judas, these forces have plotted to prevent the Light that has come into the world from carrying out its redeeming work for the forgiveness of sins.

Jesus is fully aware of the betrayal that is about to take place. In response to this ominous drama, he rises from his place and initiates an action of humble service. Reading this passage in the context of its eucharistic worship, the believing community would be challenged to identify (both individually and as a whole) those areas where darkness has penetrated its own life. Conscious of the various foibles and character flaws of Jesus' closest disciples, they would be led to reflect on their own inner capacity to betray, deny, or even doubt the presence of Jesus in their midst. Occurring as it does in the midst of the first Eucharist, the washing of the feet must be interpreted in the context of the worship of the believing community. Outside of this context it would lose much of the power that it holds over the creative imagination of the church at prayer.

2. Jesus Lays Aside His Garments (v. 4). During the meal, Jesus rises from his place and lays aside his garments. This seemingly small detail would not have gone unnoticed by the believing community. Such a gesture would have been seen as an expression of servitude by those who witnessed it. Their astonishment must have been palpable. Jesus, their Master and Teacher, puts his robes aside and relates to his disciples not as their superior or even as their equal, but as an inferior.

Jesus may very well have removed his garments for a very practical reason (e.g., not to soil them while performing a servile action). The believing community for which this passage was intended, however, would easily have seen in this gesture a symbolic expression of the humiliation of the Divine Word that took place in the incarnation (Jn 1:14; Phil 2:6–8). The believing community also would have easily made the connection between Jesus "laying aside" his garments and the earlier description of Jesus as the Good Shepherd, who "lays down" his life for his sheep (Jn 10:11, 15, 17, 18; in fact, John uses the same verb for both actions), and with the continuation of that process in the Eucharist, where Jesus becomes the living bread who gives his flesh for the life of the world (Jn 6:51). To follow the analogy through, Jesus, who "…had come from God and was going to God" (v. 3), must begin his exaltation with yet another divine humiliation. When seen in this light, his laying aside of his garments at the Last Supper anticipates a later moment when they will be forcibly taken from him (Jn 19:23–24), and he will be left to die hanging from a cross between two thieves (Jn 19:17–18).

3. Jesus Girds Himself with a Towel (v. 4). If it is through the Eucharist that the believing community participates in Jesus' humiliation and exaltation, it is through a life of committed service that the community becomes a visible expression of his ongoing presence in the world. After putting aside his garments, Jesus girds himself with a towel, giving his disciples a clear indication that he is about to perform some menial task, something usually reserved for a household servant or a slave. His intentions are slowly becoming evident, and at least one of the disciples is beginning to feel uneasy about what is about to take place (v. 6).

The towel is an instrument of cleaning. Jesus will use it to dry his disciples' feet, a common enough task given the dusty roads and pathways of first-century Palestine, but far beneath the dignity of a rabbi or teacher such as Jesus. The towel is also an instrument of preparation. By girding himself with it, Jesus readies himself for a necessary but unpalatable task of daily life. He surprises his disciples by taking on this lowly task and, through it, by teaching them in a forceful way about the meaning of discipleship. When reading this verse, the Christian community is encouraged to identify and then ready itself for the humble tasks of service that it must take on for the sake of Christ.

4. Jesus Pours Water in a Basin (v. 5). Once he has girded himself with the towel, Jesus proceeds to pour some water into a basin. The Gospel of John is noted for the various levels of meaning that the evangelist is able to evoke in his text. Here, the action of Jesus pouring water into a basin possesses strong baptismal overtones. At baptism we are immersed into the passion, death, and resurrection of Jesus and become incorporated into his body. As a result, we receive the capacity to move away from a life of egoism and self-centeredness and to live in a way that is oriented toward the love of God and neighbor. This sacramental action is first and foremost an action of Christ. By accentuating this small detail of Jesus pouring water into a basin, the evangelist reminds his audience that the eucharistic action provides them with an opportunity to recommit themselves to their baptismal promises. The step-by-step, almost ritualistic description of Jesus' actions highlights their underlying sacral character. When reading this text, the Christian community is called to remember the baptismal context of every eucharistic celebration. It is only because they have been immersed by baptism into Jesus' paschal mystery that they are able to partake of the real food and drink of Jesus' body and blood (Jn 6:54).

5. *Jesus Washes and Dries His Disciples' Feet (v. 5)*. Jesus' preparations are not ends in themselves, but have a clear and obvious purpose. After he has made the necessary preparations, he proceeds to wash and dry the feet of his disciples. The evangelist leaves his audience to imagine the caked dirt and sweaty stench that the disciples have accumulated on their feet that day from the dusty environs of Jerusalem.

It is interesting to note, however, that such washing was typically performed as one entered a house so that none of the dust would be carried in. Jesus' cleansing of his disciples' feet during their last meal together might have one of two possible meanings. On the one hand, there may have been an oversight in protocol when they entered the upper room and Jesus is taking upon himself a task that should have been performed much earlier. On the other hand, he could be making the point that, in sharing this Last Supper, they have crossed a new threshold, one from which there was no turning back and which would carry them into the kingdom. When hearing this verse read aloud in the context of the liturgical assembly, the believing community could easily have recognized that participating in the eucharistic action involved crossing a threshold to the sacred and that doing so also meant looking out for the unmet needs of others.

6. *Jesus Converses with Peter (vv. 6–11)*. In carrying out this symbolic washing Jesus also has to deal with the astonishment of his disciples. When Peter's turn comes for his feet to be washed, he protests that he will never allow his Lord and Master to wash his feet. His objections to Jesus' action stem from a fundamental misunderstanding of the meaning of discipleship.

Rather than reprimand this headstrong and outspoken disciple, Jesus engages him in conversation. He tells Peter that he will understand at a later time the reasons for his Master's strange, seemingly unwarranted actions. When Peter continues his protestations, Jesus tells him that he can have no part of him unless he permits him to wash his feet. Only then does Peter relent and permit Jesus to perform his humble act of service.

When hearing these verses read aloud in the liturgical assembly, the Christian community would see the importance of dialogue and conversation in resolving uncertainties about the mysterious action of Christ in its life. Dialogue with Christ is a simple metaphor for prayer. Those, like

Peter, with roles of leadership in the Christian community have a special obligation to bring their questions, doubts, and protestations to the Lord in prayer. Only in this way will they eventually come to understand the meaning of the Lord's action in their lives and what is being asked of them in the task of discipleship.

7. Jesus Teaches His Disciples (vv. 12–20). After his conversation with Peter, Jesus continues his task of washing his disciples' feet. When he has finished, he puts his garments back on and returns to his place at table. He then proceeds to teach them at length about the meaning of what they have just experienced. Central to his message is the call to service: "So if I, your Lord and Teacher, have washed your feet, you also ought to wash one another's feet. For I have set you an example, that you also should do as I have done to you" (vv. 14–15). Also present in his teaching is the idea that Jesus' ministry will be continued in those he sends: "Very truly, I tell you, whoever receives one whom I send receives me; and whoever receives me receives him who sent me" (v. 20). Conscious that the events of his upcoming passion and death are about to unfold, Jesus consciously depicts his life in terms of humble service. His disciples witness this drama of servanthood unfolding before their eyes.

Upon hearing these words in the liturgical assembly, the believing community is called to recognize the important place that teaching has in the life of the community. It would also be asked to see the importance of having this same drama unfold in their own lives: "servants are not greater than their master, nor are messengers greater than the one who sent them" (v. 16).

These seven points show how the author of John's gospel incorporates a call to service into the very heart of Jesus' last meal with his disciples. The full force of the meaning of this symbolic washing comes through only when it is viewed in the context of the strong eucharistic overtones woven into its textual fabric and which would have resonated deeply in the hearts of the audience for which it was originally intended. The power of this symbolic washing remains strong even to this day. One cannot read it or experience it in a liturgical setting without sensing the freshness of its message and the challenge that it presents to all who claim to be following in Jesus' footsteps.

Conclusion

Someone once described the Gospel of John as a work written by a con-templative explicitly for a contemplative community. Whatever truth there may be in such a claim, our study of the account of Jesus washing the feet of his disciples has shown that the evangelist has taken great pains to weave a variety of important, highly symbolic themes into a dramatic narrative about the Last Supper. The community that would best appreci-ate these latent spiritual motifs would be that which could deeply ponder the words of the gospel in order to distinguish the various layers of mean-ing present in the text and make relevant adaptations to the lives of its members. Regardless of whether it would actually describe itself in this way, such a community would be eminently contemplative in its approach to life, to the Christian faith, and especially to the Eucharist.

The importance of the connection between the Eucharist and the wash-ing of the disciples' feet should not be downplayed. The latter takes place during the Last Supper, an account that itself occurs at the very hinge of gospel's diptych structure between "The Book of Signs" and "The Book of Glory." As such, it holds a vital place in the unfolding of one of the evan-gelist's most significant themes—Christian love as the call to service. In one sense, everything in John's gospel—from the smallest of Jesus' signs to his greatest exaltation—can be seen as leading up to, embracing, or pre-senting an elaborate exposition of this one central motif. For this reason, it makes perfect sense that the evangelist would situate the Last Supper at the structural center of his work and that the washing of the feet would provide a potent metaphor for what was taking place both then and in the rest of Christ's redemptive action.

Even today, the close bond between Eucharist and service in John's gospel challenges us to ponder the action of Jesus in our own liturgical celebrations and to ask ourselves whether we are truly following in our Master's footsteps. Doing so means fostering a contemplative attitude toward life so that we will be able to read the signs of the Lord's presence in our midst and respond to the genuine needs of those around us. Doing so also means confronting the darkness in our lives (both as individuals and a community) and engaging the Lord in heartfelt prayer. Most of all, it means considering the community and all of its members as heralds of the gospel and servants of those in need. Only then will we become what Jesus, at this very moment, intends us to be, an authentic sign of his presence in the world and a "living parable" in the ongoing tale of the book of his glory.

Reflection Questions

• What meaning do you find in Jesus' washing the feet of his disciples? Is it merely a one-time gesture or does it touch something at the very heart of what it means to be a follower of Jesus?

• How is this humble gesture of service tied to the call to discipleship? In what ways do you live out that call?

• How is that call tied to the celebration of the Eucharist?

• In what ways do you need to humble yourself before others? In what ways are you called to serve others? In what ways are you called receive such gestures of humility and service from others?

• Does the Christian community to which you belong need to humble itself in any way? Is it being called to serve others in a particular way? Who are those others? In what ways is it called to receive such gestures of humility and service from others?

FACET SEVEN

Eating with Jesus

A Dialogue at Daybreak

Gathered there together were Simon Peter, Thomas called the Twin, Nathanael of Cana in Galilee, the sons of Zebedee, and two others of his disciples. Simon Peter said to them, "I am going fishing." They said to him, "We will go with you." They went out and got into the boat, but that night they caught nothing. Just after daybreak, Jesus stood on the beach; but the disciples did not know that it was Jesus. Jesus said to them, "Children, you have no fish, have you?" They answered him, "No." He said to them, "Cast the net to the right side of the boat, and you will find some." So they cast it, and now they were not able to haul it in because there were so many fish. (Jn 21:2–6)

Fishing is both a recreational activity and a profession. When I was a boy I used to look forward to those days when I could escape to a nearby lake and go catfishing with my makeshift bamboo pole. The morning ritual seemed almost suspended in time. The meditative walk down to the water, choosing a spot, readying my pole with hook and bait, and the repetitive casting of my line in and out of the water quieted my thoughts and brought perspective to my life. I didn't always catch something, but I found it relaxing and almost always came home with a good story about the nibbles I felt, how I landed my catch, or the big one that got away.

Many of Jesus' early followers were fishermen by trade who spent long, backbreaking hours in their boats and often had little to show for their labors. For them it was not recreation, but painstaking work that required all of their muscle as well as their undivided attention. Still, fishing was in their blood. Because they felt at home on the water, it would not be unusual for them to set out in their boats during difficult moments in their lives to let the rituals of their trade work the tensions from their bones and soothe their troubled minds.

One such instance took place at the Sea of Tiberias and was the occasion of one of Jesus' post-resurrectional appearances. Wanting to clear his mind from the tumultuous events surrounding Jesus' recent passage from this life, Peter suddenly declares that he is going fishing. The disciples who were with him decide to join him, and they all end up fishing together in a single boat for much of the night. When daybreak comes they have nothing at all to show for their efforts, until a stranger calls out to them from the shore and instructs them to cast their nets one more time on the starboard side of their boat. They do so, perhaps even grudgingly, but the result is not only one of the biggest catches of their lives, but also a story of an encounter with the risen Lord that would be told and retold for generations to come.

We too have a story to tell. It may not be as dramatic as the one we have just heard, but it has been given to us by God and is continuing to unfold in our lives. God reveals himself to us in many ways: in the circumstances of daily life, in our hearts, in our friends, in our experience of community, in the Scriptures, in our celebration of the sacraments—and especially in the Eucharist. These experiences are similar to Jesus' post-resurrectional appearances to his disciples, but also very different. While they are not to be equated with these foundational revelatory moments of the Christian faith, they nevertheless possess many interesting parallels with the narrative recollections of these experiences in the gospels. A meditative reading of the account of Peter's fishing exploits and Jesus' appearance to his disciples on the shore of the Sea of Tiberias (Jn 21:1–23) bears this out.

Some Important Background

Before examining this important post-resurrectional account, it is important for us to remember the complex nature of the fourth gospel. We need to remember that the Jesus of the fourth gospel is perceived to be continuous in his pre-incarnational, earthly, and post-resurrectional states. To encounter the human in him thus leads necessarily to an encounter with the divine—and vice versa.

John's account of Jesus' post-resurrectional appearance to his disciples on the shore of the Sea of Tiberias (21:1f) brings the added complexity of its being a second ending to the gospel (see Jn 20:30–31). This appendix may very well have circulated as an independent post-resurrectional account before it was used to close out the larger Johannine narrative. One reason for its being added may well have been the way it resonated with the experience of the believing community of its day. If this is so, it follows that we too should read it with an awareness of the possible relevance it may have for our own experience of Jesus in our daily lives.

Encountering Jesus on the Shore

The account includes seven distinct (albeit related) narrative movements: (1) a failed nighttime fishing venture by some of Jesus' closest disciples (vv. 1–3), (2) their change in fortune resulting from their dialogue at daybreak with a man standing on the shore (vv. 4–6), (3) the recognition by the beloved disciple that the man they are talking to is the Lord (v. 7a), (4) the response of Peter and the other disciples (vv. 7b–8), (5) their eating a meal with Jesus around a charcoal fire (vv. 9–14), (6) an extended dialogue between the Lord and Peter (vv. 15–19), and (7) some concluding remarks about the vocation of the beloved disciple (vv. 20–23). A close look at each of these movements may reveal some startling similarities to our own experience.

1. Gone Fishing (vv. 1–3). At the outset of the story we are told that Simon Peter, along with Thomas, Nathanael, Zebedee's sons, and two other disciples have gathered in Galilee at the shore of the Sea of Tiberias. Simon Peter decides to go fishing, and the others resolve to join him. We are also told that they work all through the night and are unable to catch anything.

This first movement bears a marked resemblance to the Synoptic accounts of Jesus' calling of his first disciples (Mk 1:16–20; Mt 4:18–22; and especially Lk 5:1–11). By virtue of this association, it conveys a deeper understanding of the call to discipleship. In the Synoptic accounts, Jesus tells his disciples to leave their nets because he will make them fishers of men. In the Johannine account, the disciples have taken up their nets again, this time after the events of Easter Sunday. Because it occurs in the context of a post-resurrectional encounter, their fishing can easily be taken to signify the early missionary activity of Christ's disciples. The fact that those who join Simon Peter in this effort include both those who were known to be fishermen by trade (Zebedee's sons, Mk 1:19; Mt 4:21; Lk 5:10) and those who were not (Thomas and Nathanael are nowhere in the gospels directly identified as fishermen) further strengthens this assumption. The two unnamed disciples (v. 2), moreover, add an element of anonymity to the group and help us to identify all the more with the early missionary endeavors of Simon Peter and his companions.

These verses remind us that all of Christ's followers—past, present, and future—are called to join in the missionary activity of the church, symbolized in this and other gospel stories by the small fishing boat that has set out to sea (see Mk 4:35–41; Mt 8:23–27; Lk 8:22–25). In addition, two specific traits stand out about the nature of this missionary activity. The first concerns the weakness of those chosen to carry it out, as exemplified at various points in the gospel narratives by Peter's denial (Jn 18:12–27), Thomas' doubt (Jn 20:19–29), Nathanael's suspicion (Jn 1:46), and, at least as far as the Synoptic tradition is concerned, James' and John's presumption (Mk 10:35–40; Mt 20:20–23). The second is the disciples' failure to achieve anything through their own efforts, as indicated by their empty nets after an entire night of intense labor. These same traits remain as true for us today as they did for Jesus' earliest disciples.

2. A Dialogue at Daybreak (vv. 4–6). The disciples' fortune changes only with the break of dawn and the heavily symbolic movement from darkness to light. Standing on the shore and watching them go about their work, Jesus engages them in conversation and asks if they have caught anything. Not recognizing who he is, they inform him that their efforts have thus far been fruitless. Jesus responds by telling them that they will be sure to catch something if they drop their nets on the starboard side of the boat. On following his advice they catch so many fish that they can barely haul in their net.

At this point in the story it is important to note that Jesus takes the initiative to speak with his disciples and that he gives them sound advice about where they should fish. Although his knowledge of the whereabouts of the fish may come from his miraculous powers, it is not impossible that Jesus could see from the shore with his naked eye something that his disciples could not see from their boat at close range. In any case, Jesus' advice is listened to, followed, and greatly benefited from.

It is also important to note that he does this from shore. An expanse of water separates Jesus from his disciples, about a hundred yards as we are informed later on in the tale (v. 8). The meeting of land and sea here symbolizes the meeting of two worlds and can easily be understood as a threshold to the sacred. Jesus calling out to his disciples represents an invitation for them to step across the boundaries of everyday life for an intimate encounter with the divine.

These elements of the story remind us that the missionary efforts of the disciples succeed only because of Jesus' active guidance. It also reminds us that, while the Jesus of the post-resurrectional accounts is continuous with the earthly Jesus, something has changed in him that prevents his disciples from recognizing him (see Lk 24:16; Jn 20:14). The expanse of water separating Jesus from his disciples brings to mind a similar distance in our own experience of God. To enter into this water is to embrace the way of Jesus in its entirety. It refers not only to baptism by water but also, as indicated by Jesus' conversation with Peter later on in the story (vv. 15–19), to the way of martyrdom (i.e., what later came to be referred to as baptism by blood). The latter would have great significance for Christians living during a time of persecution. It reminds us of the true cost of discipleship, one that embraces the cross as a true means of liberation for oneself and others.

3. The Moment of Recognition (v. 7b). As the disciples are tending to their haul of fish, the disciple Jesus loved suddenly realizes who the man standing on the shore really is. "It is the Lord!" he cries out to Peter. Although his identity is unknown, the beloved disciple has often been associated with John, the brother of James and son of Zebedee. Some scholars disagree, saying the beloved disciple is merely a symbol for the perfect disciple; still others claim he refers to another close disciple of Jesus or possibly a minor, lesser known New Testament personage (v. 20).

Regardless of his identity, this disciple shares a close relationship with Peter throughout the gospel and is often contrasted with him. Peter denies Christ (18:15–18, 25–27); the beloved disciple follows Christ to the foot of the cross (19:25–27). Both set out together to verify the news about the empty tomb (20:1–10). The beloved disciple runs ahead and peers in (20:4), but does not enter until Peter arrives (20:6). In the present story, the beloved disciple recognizes Jesus and shouts the news to Peter (7b) Throughout this gospel, the life of one seems inextricably tied to that of the other: Peter is presented as a leader and man of action; the beloved disciple is presented as a contemplative and someone especially cherished by Jesus. In the present story, it is entirely fitting that the beloved disciple should be the one to recognize the stranger on the shore as Jesus, the risen Lord. This recognition of Jesus, however, comes not from an inborn ability of his own, but by way of gift. The beloved disciple recognizes Jesus only because his Master has revealed himself to him. His witness hastens, but does not cause, a similar recognition on the part of the other disciples.

The beloved disciple's role in the story underscores the importance for all Christians to foster a contemplative attitude toward life. It is also important to note that the gift of contemplation does not contradict the life of pastoral action and missionary activity, but actually sustains it. John, the beloved disciple, and Peter, the Rock, play two very different (albeit closely related) roles in the building up of God's kingdom. To place them in conflict with one another or to treat them as if one had absolutely nothing to do with the other, misses one of the most fundamental points of the gospel message.

4. Peter's Response (vv. 7b–8). After hearing that the stranger on the beach is the Lord, the half-naked Peter quickly wraps a cloak around himself and plunges into the water. As he makes his way toward his Master the others remain in the boat in order to tow the net with its abundant catch of fish toward the shore some one hundred yards away.

Peter's quick, seemingly impulsive response separates him from the other disciples. He does not enter the water without thinking, however, for he has enough of his wits about him to throw some clothes on in order to greet his Master in an appropriate, dignified manner. Although he is not the first to recognize Jesus, he is the first to greet him—and to do so with respect. His entrance into the water points to the zeal for Christ that certain individuals are given from age to age for the good of the church. By jumping into the water Peter affirms his love for Christ and undergoes a kind of baptism. From a symbolic standpoint, this action anticipates Jesus' speech to him about martyrdom (the ultimate witness for Christ, vv. 18–19) and indicates the prominent role that Peter's death played in sustaining the faith of the early church. Is this the Rock upon which Jesus promises to build his church?

This part of the narrative reminds us that, while all are called to make their way to Christ, some are called to do so in an extraordinary way. By throwing himself into the water, Peter throws all caution to the wind and does whatever he has to do to make his way to Jesus as soon as possible. The example of Peter causes us to examine ourselves and to determine the extent to which we have been too careful or reserved in our expression of the faith. It is one thing to make one's way toward Christ when we are unchallenged and in relative safety, and quite another to offer him the ultimate witness of our faith. That is not to say, however, that one form of witness is better than another. All is gift. In the end, all the disciples arrive on shore and warm themselves around a fire prepared for them by the Lord.

5. Eating with Jesus (vv. 9–14). When the disciples land their boat they find Jesus preparing a meal of bread and fish cooked over a charcoal fire. He asks them to bring over some of the fish that they have just caught. Peter goes to the boat and hauls the net ashore with its huge catch of fish—153 in all. Despite the great number of the fish in it, the net has not broken. Jesus then invites his disciples to refresh themselves around the fire and to partake of the food he has prepared for them. No one presumes to ask him who he is; they all know he is the Lord. Jesus shares his meal with them by taking the bread and giving it to them and then doing the same with the fish. We are then told that this was the third time that Jesus appeared to his disciples after his resurrection.

This scene is full of eucharistic imagery. The bread and fish remind us of the miracle of the multiplication of the loaves and fish, a story present in both John and the Synoptics (Jn 6:1–15 ; Mt 14:13–21; Mk 6:32–44; Lk 9:10–17), and which itself, as we have already explored, was often understood as a foreshadowing of the Eucharist. The sense of community participation is also evident when Jesus invites his disciples to bring some of the fish they have just caught so that it they too could be cooked and eaten. The charcoal fire signifies both the sacrificial element of the meal and the life of the Spirit that makes the eucharistic celebration possible. The setting, the shore of a sea, indicates that this sacred meal takes place at the threshold or meeting place between two worlds. The whole event, moreover, transpires in the presence of Christ, who presides over the meal and gives it its special sacral character. The enigmatic number of fish may refer to the various species of fish generally believed, at that time, to have been created by God. If this is so, it affirms the gospel's claim that all are called to hear Christ's message of salvation and partake of his life-giving body.

Jesus' hospitality to his disciples dominates this part of the narrative. It reminds us that the celebration of the Eucharist is meant to be a life-giving, nourishing event, one that celebrates community, life in the Spirit, and the encounter with the sacred. It also recalls the central role that Jesus plays in each eucharistic celebration. Even though we do not see him physically, we believe in his presence in our midst and, with the disciples, have no need to ask him to identify himself.

6. *The Dialogue with Peter (vv. 15–19).* After the meal Jesus turns to Peter and three times asks him if he loves him. Each time Peter replies that he does, to which Jesus responds with the words, "Feed, my sheep." Peter is hurt after Jesus' third interrogation and makes an emphatic statement of his love. Jesus responds with the same command and then goes into an extended statement about what the future holds for him. If Peter, as a young man, could fasten his belt as he pleased and go where he wished, the time will come when he will stretch out his arms and another will tie him fast and carry him off against his will. A parenthetical statement tells us that Jesus is here specifically referring to the kind of death Peter will one day undergo. Jesus ends the conversation with the simple command for Peter to follow him. In its present context, this directive points to the way of the cross and the laying down of one's life for the sake of Christ.

This part of the narrative parallels the earlier passage in the Gospel of John where Peter denies Christ three times (18:12–27); both scenes, in fact, take place before a charcoal fire (18:18; 21:9). Peter, who abandoned Christ in his time of need, and who, unlike the beloved disciple, did not follow his Master to the foot of the cross, is now being given the opportunity to proclaim his love for Jesus. Although it is quite likely that Peter had already repented of his sin in private, there is something very concrete, very public, almost sacramental in the way Jesus calls upon him to affirm his love and devotion. The interrogation is done for Peter's sake. It brings the process of forgiveness to completion and enables him to fully accept Christ's unfailing love.

When going through this part of the story, we get the sense that, with each acclamation of love and affection, each act of denial is dramatically undone. As a result of Peter's strong affirmation of love for his Lord and Master, Jesus now gives him the opportunity not only to follow him to the foot of the cross, but also to embrace it. By dying a martyr's death, Peter will follow the Lord in a way he never before thought he was capable of doing. Strengthened by the Eucharist and by the fellowship of the early Christian community, he will tend the flock entrusted to his care with every ounce of his being. His own death will confirm his love for Christ and Christ's body, the church. Peter, one might say, is called to make Jesus' words his own: "I am the good shepherd. The good shepherd lays down his life for the sheep" (Jn 10:11). Those who follow in the steps and assume the pastoral responsibilities of this Rock must, in some way, seek to do the same. In a similar way, every believer is called to lay down his or her life for their friends (Jn 15:13).

7. The Beloved Disciple (vv. 20–23). The concluding verses of the scene focus on the fate of the beloved disciple. After hearing of the path he himself is to travel, Peter asks Jesus what will happen to his young companion. Jesus responds that it should not concern him. Peter's business is simply to follow Christ. It should not matter if Jesus desires the beloved disciple to remain alive until he returns. As a result a report circulates that this disciple would not see death. The evangelist, however, is quick to point out that Jesus never says anything definitive about the life or death of the beloved disciple.

This part of the narrative is much more about Peter than the beloved disciple. Given an insight into the particular path his following of Christ will take, Peter is now tempted to compare himself with others. He looks at the beloved disciple and inquires if he too is going to be asked to make the ultimate sacrifice. Jesus takes Peter to task for this remark, telling him that he has no business inquiring into the path another must walk. Peter, the Rock, must follow where Jesus leads him; the beloved disciple must follow his own calling. The important thing is to keep one's eyes on Christ and to follow. Comparing one's walk of faith with another's can easily become a distraction and even detrimental to the life of discipleship.

Anyone in the Christian community can make the same mistake. We are called not to compare ourselves with others, but to love them and to have compassion toward them. The closing verses of this post-resurrectional account remind us that, even when we are in the presence of Jesus and discover the path we are called to walk, old attitudes, habits, and ways of relating still linger within us. Peter's inquiry about the beloved disciple reminds us that even saints are in need of continual conversion. To become holy we need only to take Jesus' simple words to heart. If we concern ourselves only with following him, we shall have nothing to worry about. No matter what happens, all shall be well.

Conclusion

Although our experience is different from Peter and the disciples, it is also very similar. Their experience of Jesus on the shore of the Sea of Tiberias has much to teach us. In seven narrative movements the account reveals a wide spectrum of experiences with which we can easily identify. Hard work ending in failure, fruitful encounters with strangers, moments of recognition, decisive impulses for change, hospitality, community, experiencing the call to follow, confronting old habits—these are just some of the experiences that resonate within us when we give this important gospel text a careful, meditative reading.

More important, at the center of this post-resurrectional account is the meal of bread and fish that Jesus shares with his disciples. Not only does it appear in the very middle of the text (vv. 9–12), but a study of the narrative movement of the story as a whole reveals that everything leads up to it and flows from it. For the communities in which this passage circulated—be it independently or as the second ending of John's gospel—the implications were clear. The risen Lord was present in, and to be experienced in, the breaking of the bread. It was for this reason that the celebration of the Eucharist was such a central focus of their lives. To it, they could bring the wide range of their experiences (of whatever type) and find renewed hope and meaning as they broke bread together and passed the cup. In commemorating the celebration of the Last Supper, they believed that Jesus, the Living Bread, actually came into their midst. It was from this deep encounter of faith with the living God that they gained deeper insights into the paths they were called to walk and the traps they were cautioned to avoid.

Like the disciples who meet Jesus on the shore, every community of believers is a diverse blend of characters. When we read about Peter, Thomas, Nathanael, James, and John (and let us not forget the two nameless disciples), we are reminded that our own denials, our own doubts, our own suspicions, our own presumptions, and even our own anonymity can and will be transformed by Christ—if only we will let him. Jesus knows us through and through and has a special name for each one of us. And our strengths, whatever they may be, are acknowledged, confirmed, deepened, and elevated as a result of our encounter with the Lord in the breaking of the bread.

As a result of their continued participation in the breaking of the bread, Peter moved from denial to martyrdom and the beloved disciple from presumption to the heights of contemplation. The same can and will be said of us. It is in the Eucharist where we meet Christ, encounter his love for us, and discover the path he is calling us to walk.

Reflection Questions

• Have you ever had the experience of hard work ending in failure? If so, what did you learn from the experience? In what way did it challenge you or help you to grow?

• What fruitful encounters with strangers have you had in your life? What do you remember most about them? How did they affect you?

• How have you experienced hospitality? Forgiveness? A call to change? What do such simple experiences tell you about your faith? Were you able to recognize the presence of the Lord in any them? Were you able to greet him in those moments and respond to him from your heart? What do such experiences tell you about the mission of the church and the call to discipleship?

After Pentecost

The Life of Discipleship

They devoted themselves to the apostles' teaching and fellowship, to the breaking of bread and the prayers. Awe came upon everyone, because many wonders and signs were being done by the apostles. All who believed were together and had all things in common; they would sell their possessions and goods and distribute the proceeds to all, as any had need. Day by day, as they spent much time together in the temple, they broke bread at home and ate their food with glad and generous hearts, praising God and having the goodwill of all the people. And day by day the Lord added to their number those who were being saved. (Acts 2:42–47)

Do you consider yourself a disciple of Jesus? I would like to consider myself one. Unfortunately, I do not always live up to what one would normally expect of a disciple. I sometimes feel weak and cowardly, not able to stand up for my beliefs and all too often willing to go with the majority opinion, regardless of whether it is right or wrong. I find some solace in knowing that the apostles themselves were a weak and motley crew of followers. Just go down the list and you would be hard pressed to find someone who did not eventually desert, deny, or betray Jesus.

After Pentecost, however, Jesus' followers were transformed into a tightly knit body of believers who not only understood what it meant to be a disciple, but were also willing to pay the price. What is the cost of discipleship? There is no doubt in Jesus' mind: "If any want to become my followers, let them deny themselves and take up their cross daily and follow me" (Lk 9:23). What could be clearer? The trouble is, it is very difficult to follow these instructions—at least for me. I am constantly making mistakes and need to learn (and relearn) their meaning every day. Only prayer, the power of God's Spirit, and the experience of breaking bread with others in community prevent me from giving up. Much the same, I believe, was true for the experience and practice of the primitive Christian community.

After the coming of the Holy Spirit at Pentecost, the primitive Christian community at Jerusalem maintained its identity through its devotion "…to the apostles' teaching and fellowship, to the breaking of bread and the prayers" (Acts 2:42). These four practices set these early believers apart from the rest of the Jewish world and gave them a sense of unity and cohesiveness that made a deep impression on their growing self-perception. Although problems arose that would challenge and, at times, deeply shake this strong sense of identity, the Christian community would always look to its formative experience of faith as a time when the Holy Spirit was leading it in a powerful, almost palpable, way. A look at the circumstances surrounding the rise of this early fellowship of believers reveals a concerted effort to live a radical life of discipleship rooted in the teachings of Jesus and motivated by the hope in his imminent return.

The Coming of the Spirit

The accounts of the coming of the Holy Spirit vary in length and detail. Mark's gospel makes no mention of it whatsoever. In Matthew's gospel the Spirit's coming is simply presumed when Jesus commissions the apostles to make disciples of all nations, baptizing "in the name of the Father and of the Son and of the Holy Spirit" (Mt 28:19). In John's gospel Jesus breathes on his disciples when he gives them the power to forgive sins (see Jn 20:22–23). Luke/Acts provides an extended description of the coming of the Spirit to the disciples as "a sound like the rush of a violent wind" and as "tongues as of fire" resting above their heads, giving them the power "to speak in other languages" (see Acts 2:1–4). The reason for this diversity stems from the varying theological concerns of the evangelists and the particular aspect of the Christ event each wishes to emphasize in his narrative. When taken together, they affirm the intimate relationship between the descent of the Spirit and the other aspects of the paschal mystery.

The account of the coming of the Holy Spirit in Luke/Acts is especially significant because it offers many important insights into how the primitive Christian community acted in the aftermath of Jesus' return to the Father. With Jesus no longer with them in his tangible, transformed state, the apostles returned to the upper room, where they devoted themselves to constant prayer and awaited the coming of the Spirit (see Acts 1:4, 14). During this time they decided to select someone to take the place of Judas Iscariot. After nominating two men, they prayed to God for guidance, drew lots, and in this way welcomed Matthias as one of the Twelve (see Acts 1:15–26).

This process of selection involved active deliberation, spiritual discernment, and an element of chance. It demonstrates the apostles' great trust in God and their willingness to place the most important decisions about their future in the hands of Providence. It also provides an insight into the way the earliest followers of Jesus initially thought they should carry on in their Master's absence. With the death of Judas, it was quite natural for them to want to replenish their ranks so that they could maintain one of the few structures established by Jesus during his life on earth. The twelve apostles represented twelve judges for the twelve tribes of Israel and indicated that Jesus' message was meant for the whole of Israel.

With the outpouring of the Holy Spirit on the feast of Pentecost, the apostles and those with them in the upper room were empowered to make a bold proclamation of the Easter message. Whatever the outward expressions of the Spirit's presence in their midst, the inward transformation that went on in the hearts and minds of these early followers cannot be questioned. It was the Spirit, and no one else, who changed this small group of believers into the dynamic body that would reshape the spiritual landscape of the world. With Peter as their leading voice, this body of believers proclaimed Jesus as the long-awaited Messiah and encouraged their listeners to repent and be baptized. On that one day alone more than three thousand accepted their message, were baptized, and were added to their fold (see Acts 2:14–41).

The Primitive Community

The gift of the Spirit at Pentecost made possible the kind of community life envisioned in the early chapters of the Acts of the Apostles (see Acts 2:42–47; 4:32–35; 5:12–16). The practices listed there present a dynamic vision of the demands of Christian discipleship for the time and were held in high regard by believers. That is not to say that the early Christian community at Jerusalem did not experience any growing pains. As later episodes in the Acts of the Apostles attest, a number of deep personal and communal tensions greatly impeded the primitive community's attempt to live out this radical vision of discipleship. The most blatant of these difficulties concerned the distribution of wealth (Acts 5:1–11), the relationships between Hebrew- and Greek-speaking believers (Acts 6:1–2), and the binding force of the Mosaic Law (Acts 15:1–4). These troubles forced the primitive community of believers to reassess its self-understanding and the scope of its missionary outreach. The result was an opening up of its requisites for membership that extended from the center of temple worship in Jerusalem to the various communities of the Jewish diaspora, and to the Gentiles of the Hellenic world and beyond.

In the midst of these and other tensions, the four characteristic practices of the primitive community at Jerusalem take on greater relevance for the church's developing self-understanding. A look at each of these practices will draw out some of the implications of this claim.

1. The Instruction of the Apostles. With Jesus ascended to his rightful place at the Father's right hand, the early community of believers needed reliable leaders to guide and instruct them in the ways of their newborn faith. It was quite natural for them to turn to the apostles, those men specifically chosen by Jesus to represent the universality of his message for the twelve tribes of Israel and later commissioned by him to carry his message of salvation to the ends of the earth. After the death of Judas Iscariot, the apostles, as just noted, reconstituted their number to twelve through the election of Matthias, an action that revealed their desire to continue the prophetic proclamation of their Master and to do so through the very structures that he himself had instituted. These structures of governance would adapt to the changing needs and circumstances of the expanding church and, in the course of the next century and a half, would evolve into a hierarchical structure of bishops, priests, and deacons.

The instruction of the apostles had special significance for the early community of believers. They were the ones responsible for administering the teachings of the Lord and for insuring its authenticity. Their words were received with great reverence and given special weight in all community deliberations. Important decisions concerning the life and mission of the community were referred to them. They were looked upon as having been especially chosen by Jesus to work with him during his earthly ministry in the proclamation of the coming of God's reign and also to continue this mission of teaching and preaching under the guidance of his Spirit. The members of the early Christian community listened to their testimony of the risen Lord and adhered to the teachings that flowed from it. For them, these teachings complemented the Jewish Scriptures and, when written down and collected, would evolve into a body of documents that eventually formed the New Testament canon.

2. The Communal Life. The early Christian community was a body of believers united by their faith in the risen Lord. The bonds of fellowship flowing from their deep unity of faith resulted in concrete expressions in the life of the community, the most radical sign of which was the sharing of possessions. This practice harks back to Jesus' custom of sharing a common purse with his close circle of disciples as a way of emphasizing the imminent coming of God's reign. Similar practices existed in contemporary Jewish movements such as the Essenes, where apocalyptic hopes for an imminent coming of the Messiah diminished the importance of material possessions and led to a strong emphasis on pooling the resources of the community. In the primitive Christian community this sharing of possessions took place not on isolated desert slopes, but in the winding streets and market precincts of the city. The extent of such sharing cannot be determined with accuracy, did not seem to lift the Jerusalem community out of its poverty, and may even have exacerbated the situation.

For Paul, collections of money by Hellenic Christians for the Jerusalem church were concrete signs of their fellowship (*koinonia*) with one another by virtue of being members of the Christ's body (see Gal 2:9–10). Such gestures of communion were greatly appreciated by those in need and helped ease some of the tensions between the Jewish and Gentile Christians over the place the observance of the Mosaic Law had in the daily practice of the faith. The witness of the communal life was valued highly in all areas of Christian life, but gradually became the special vocation of certain select subgroups. For much of the church's history it has been variously maintained by the active and contemplative religious orders, each of which has adapted the practice to the demands of its own charism.

3. *The Breaking of the Bread.* The Eucharist was yet another practice that bound the primitive Jerusalem together. Jesus' last meal with his disciples was commemorated by the believing community and considered by them to be a foretaste of the heavenly banquet. This celebration apparently did not interfere with their regular temple worship. Jesus' followers went daily to the temple area to pray and then returned to their homes to break bread together (Acts 2:46). The members of the primitive Christian community saw no conflict between their new found faith and the traditional practices of Jewish observance. Although tensions would arise later, their initial reaction was to look upon their new-found faith as something that complemented their Jewish heritage, but did not supplant it. The Eucharist was celebrated as a communal meal, in much the same way as the Last Supper (see Acts 2:46; Lk 22:7–13). The emphasis on celebrating it in their homes says something about the intimate nature of their gatherings and the important role that this communal meal had in building up the fellowship of believers. As Jesus' own words attest, the blessing of the bread and wine at the Last Supper was strongly identified with his body and blood (Mt 26:26; Mk 14:22–25; Lk 22:19–20). The believing community took these words seriously and strongly believed that Jesus entered their midst when they broke bread together and shared the stories of his passion, death, and resurrection. Accounts of Jesus' post-resurrection appearances taking place during the breaking of the bread (e.g., Lk 24:13–35) were listened to intently at such gatherings. It is also highly likely that the written form of these stories evolved in subtle ways to meet the needs of such liturgical settings.

The Eucharist was a central ritual of the believing community. Reflection on its meaning would, in time, draw even closer connections with Jesus' paschal mystery. As the believing community grew in numbers, the place of worship would be moved from the home to larger dwellings. To prevent abuses in celebration, the ritualistic blessing of the bread and wine was separated from the rest of the meal and would become the focal point of the worship of the Christian assembly.

4. The Prayers. After Jesus' ascension the early community of believers "...were constantly devoting themselves to prayer" (Acts 1:14). In the beginning such prayers were often modeled after Jewish prayer forms of intercession, petition, thanksgiving, and adoration—to name but a few. Many of these were written down and intended for private use. Others were put to music and incorporated into the community's baptismal and liturgical celebrations. As time went on the expanding church community began to develop a teaching on prayer that was more spontaneous and charismatic in its outlook. In his letters the apostle Paul would write of the importance of praying always: "Rejoice always, pray without ceasing, give thanks in all circumstances; for this is the will of God in Christ Jesus for you" (1 Thess 5:16–18). He also would remind his readers that prayer itself is a gift of God and that the Holy Spirit groans within us and helps us to pray: "Likewise the Spirit helps us in our weakness; for we do not know how to pray as we ought, but that very Spirit intercedes with sighs too deep for words. And God, who searches the heart, knows what is the mind of the Spirit, because the Spirit intercedes for the saints according to the will of God" (Rom 8:26–27).

Emphasis would also be given to the gifts of the Spirit for building up the body of Christ (see 1 Cor 12:1–11). Paul's most basic teaching regarding prayer was quite simple: "...no one can say 'Jesus is Lord,' except by the Holy Spirit" (1 Cor 12:3). Since the life of discipleship entailed a radical following of Christ, the expanding community of believers made a concerted effort to develop forms of prayers that were modeled on the way Jesus himself had prayed. The centrality of the eucharistic celebration for the believing community sprang mainly from Jesus' injunction to his disciples to do it in memory of him (see Lk 22:19). The Lord's Prayer (Mt 6:9–13; Lk 11:2–4) incorporates prayers of both praise and petition and came to be thought of as the Christian prayer par excellence; it was encouraged in personal prayer as well as in communal and more specifically liturgical settings. Dedication to prayer was a characteristic mark of the Christian community from the very beginning. Although the emphasis might change according to times and circumstances, its goal was always to share in an intimate relationship with the God whom Jesus referred to time and time again as "Abba, Father."

Devotion to the instructions of the apostles, fellowship, the breaking of the bread, and the prayers: these identifying characteristics of the primitive community of believers are, for many, the mainstay of the practice of Christian discipleship. They survive in one shape or another down to the present and share close ties with the universal church's own self-understanding.

The Marks of the Church

One way of asserting the continuity between the practice of discipleship in the primitive Christian community and our situation today is by noting the similarities between the characteristics described above and what have traditionally been termed "the four marks of the church." The Nicene Creed asserts the existence of "one holy catholic and apostolic Church," a belief that has been affirmed time and again in the church's liturgical prayer. But this assertion carries with it more than merely a doctrinal affirmation about the mystery of Christ's body, the church: *lex orandi, lex credendi, lex vivendi:* the law of prayer, is the law of belief, is the law of living. Every doctrinal formulation has certain ethical implications associated with it—and vice versa. When applied to the four marks of the church, such an assertion means that what pertains to the very nature of the church has serious ramifications for the practice of Christian discipleship. To say that the church is one, holy, catholic, and apostolic necessarily implies that we act accordingly.

The characteristics of the primitive faith community at Jerusalem shed some revealing light on what such action might entail. The oneness of the church, for example, represents not so much a goal that has already been reached but a vision that is constantly being worked toward and implemented. It requires that striving toward fellowship and communion signified by the *koinonia* of the early Christian community. Such dedication seeks to overcome the tensions currently being faced by the community so that a genuine unity of faith and practice might arise.

The holiness of the church requires its members to constantly seek the Lord through prayer. Holiness requires the activity of the divine and the receptiveness of the human heart. Such activity must be constant and ongoing. It is best represented by the early believers "...constantly devoting themselves to prayer" (Acts 1:14). A life of prayer is a *sine qua non* of a life of holiness. Without it, the community of faith cannot exist, let alone thrive and prosper.

The catholicity of the church affirms its universal mission and focuses on those dimensions of our lives that stress our common humanity. In the primitive community, the commitment to the common life through the sharing of possessions was a way of equalizing relations among the different social classes so that the Lord's message of the Father's unconditional love could find concrete expression in the life of the community. It also provided an important eschatological dimension to the practice of discipleship by emphasizing the relative value of the goods of the present life in the light of the world to come.

The apostolicity of the church means that its faith rests upon the testimony of the apostles. They not only witnessed the risen Lord but also were specifically commissioned by him to lead the community of believers in its maturing in, and spreading of, the faith. The primitive Christian community looked to the apostles for both instruction and leadership. In doing so it affirmed the continuity of what it believed with those who actually witnessed and thus could affirm the continuity of Jesus in his earthly and transformed states. Today the apostolic nature of the church affirms the present structures of church governance that evolved from the efforts of the apostles to proclaim a message that could adapt to changing circumstances yet remain continuous with their own experience of their Lord and Master.

These marks relate to each other in reciprocal fashion and find visible expression in the breaking of the bread. This commemoration of Jesus' last meal before his death and resurrection effects what it signifies and embraces every aspect of the paschal mystery. Since it is primarily an action of Christ, the Eucharist brings the dynamic, creative presence of the Word into the midst of the believing community. The one, holy, catholic, and apostolic nature of the faith flows from this divine/human action and ultimately returns to it.

For the primitive Christian community, the eucharistic action forged its identity as a fellowship of Christ's disciples. Breaking bread together was a way of affirming their oneness of faith in the risen Lord, their deep yearning to be with him, their expectation of his imminent return, and their respect for those he appointed in roles of leadership. The breaking of the bread was their way of both recalling the origins of their faith and anticipating the fullness of God's reign in the messianic banquet to come.

Conclusion

The four practices of the primitive community at Jerusalem gave these early believers a deep sense of belonging to one another and to the Lord. Although first seen as complementary to the usual Jewish practices of the day, these practices had great significance for the early community in their own right and would become the central focus of how the life of disciple-ship was to be lived. The primitive church at Jerusalem looked upon itself first and foremost as the community of disciples of the risen Lord. Devotion to fellowship, the prayers, the breaking of the bread, and the instruction of the apostles was the concrete way in which their desire to follow their Master was put into practice.

The practices delineated in Acts 2:42 represent some of the noblest ideals of the primitive community. Although that community did not always live up to them (see Acts 5:1–11; 6:1–2), these ideals were held up as the vision of the kind of community the Spirit of God was constantly calling them to become. Other passages from Luke/Acts corroborate this claim (see Acts 4:32–35; 5:12–16) and demonstrate how Jesus' vision of the reign of God held sway over this tiny, but fast-growing band of followers.

These same four practices are continuous with what eventually came to be known as "the four marks of the church." Like the primitive Christian community at Jerusalem, we are called to identify those practices that will mold us into a close-knit fellowship dedicated to the instruction of the apostles, the life of prayer, and the breaking of the bread. Only then can we be said to be one, holy, catholic, and apostolic. The practice of break-ing bread together is especially significant in this regard. Through our common celebration of the Eucharist, the action of Christ moves us to act as his body in the world. When one thinks of all that Jesus went through during his short time on earth, such a proposal brings greater perspective to the meaning of Christian existence and the radical call to discipleship.

Reflection Questions

• In a single sentence, how would you describe your experience of Christian community? What are the positive and negative elements of it?

• How are the four characteristics of primitive Christianity reflected in your experience of Christian community? Which of these character-istics are most important to you? How are they present in your own life?

• What do you think and feel when the church is affirmed as being one, holy, catholic, and apostolic? Are these mere abstractions or do you have a concrete experience of these traits in your own experience of Christian community?

• In what way do the four characteristics of the primitive Christian com-munity present a challenge to the church today? What would be some concrete steps that would enable your community to respond to that challenge?

One Bread, One Body

Overcoming Division

The cup of blessing that we bless, is it not a sharing in the blood of Christ? The bread that we break, is it not a sharing in the body of Christ? Because there is one bread, we who are many are one body, for we all partake of the one bread. (1 Cor 10:16–17)

Dissension among Christians is one of the great, ongoing scandals of church history. Although unity is supposed to be one of the identifying marks of the Christ's body, a candid look at relations among Christians down through the centuries reveals a sordid history of controversy, distrust, suspicion, and mutual animosity. Such discord has manifested itself among the various Christian denominations, in local parish communities, within families, and even among friends. Whatever its cause—institutional, doctrinal, ethical, personal—most of us would agree that relating in such a manner is opposed to the gospel message. How could it not be? Jesus prayed that his followers might be one (Jn 17:11). If we take an honest look at ourselves and the way we live our lives, however, we would have to admit that this prayer has not yet been answered—at least not fully.

The situation gets worse when we look at the Eucharist. This sacrament is supposed to be a celebration of Christian unity, an anticipation of the messianic banquet, a reflection of the community of love enjoyed by the saints in heaven. Down through history, however, it has often been the source of heated disputes and deep theological wrangling. Such dissension goes back even to the early days of the church. Just take a look at the early Christian community at Corinth.

When writing about the Eucharist to that troubled community, Paul refers the believers at Corinth to their formative communal experience and to the tradition that he himself received and was specifically chosen to promulgate. In doing so, he provides this struggling Christian community with a poignant call to overcome whatever divisions are affecting its daily life and worship and to live out the unity that the eucharistic meal signifies.

Paul's words have special significance for us today. If we, as a living community of faith, wish to give concrete, visible expression to the intimate bond of love existing between the Father and the Son, we must humbly ask the Lord to forgive us our sins and help us to overcome whatever keeps us apart. Ongoing rancor and distrust have no place among Christians, regardless of their denomination, and, least of all, at the table of the Lord.

The Church at Corinth: A Divided Community

Located at the southern point of the narrow isthmus connecting the large Peloponnesus peninsula to the Greek mainland, the city of Corinth was an important industrial center of the ancient Mediterranean world. Destroyed by the Romans in 146 B.C., it was rebuilt 100 years later by Julius Ceasar and eventually became the capital of the Roman province of Achaia. In the first century A.D., Corinth enjoyed a reputation as a booming commercial seaport. In Paul's time the city's inhabitants came from all over the empire. Its ethnic, cultural, and religious diversity gave it a cosmopolitan air, one that also gave rise to its reputation for loose living and sexual license.

Paul evangelized Corinth during his second missionary journey from the end of 50 to the middle of 52 A.D. In doing so, he was following his typical strategy of forming viable Christian communities in stable population centers. From these cities, he believed, the faith would eventually disseminate into the surrounding countryside. Because Corinth was a great commercial center, it also became a crossroads of innovative ideas, philosophies, and religions of every type. The fledgling Christian community established there by Paul was easily influenced by these diverse influences.

Before long, the apostle received reports of divisions within the community that centered, among others, on such issues as lawsuits, sexual misconduct, marriage, food offered to idols, and preferential treatment given during the Eucharist. To heal these divisions he wrote a series of three letters during the spring and autumn of 57 A.D.—the first of which is lost—and even paid them a personal visit to get a close, firsthand look at their troubles (see 1 Cor 5:9–13; 11:34). As the two surviving letters indicate, the church at Corinth was very dear to Paul's heart. As the founder of this struggling Christian community, he instructed them, exhorted them, and even disciplined them as a father would his young, misbehaving children.

Paul's Institution Narrative: The Larger Context

In 1 Cor 11:23–25, Paul gives us the earliest institution narrative in the New Testament. It was written a number of years before Mark's gospel and bears some marked similarities to the account in Lk 22:19–20. Although Paul claims to have received it from the Lord, he is more likely recounting for his readers elements of the apostolic tradition that he witnessed in the communal worship of the church in Antioch. It was at Antioch where the disciples of Jesus first came to be known as "Christians" and where Paul spent a year to deepen his understanding of the faith he once persecuted (see Acts 9:1–2; 11:19–26). It was from Antioch that Paul set out with Barnabas on his first missionary journey (Acts 13:1–3) and where he returned to relate all that the Lord had accomplished through his preaching (14:24–28).

Paul's description of the institution of the Eucharist (1 Cor 11:23–25) occurs in the body of the letter (1 Cor 1:10–16:18) at a point where he deals with specific problems of conduct (1 Cor 5:1–11:34). His insertion of the institution narrative in a part of his letter dealing with moral behavior may seem inappropriate to some and, at best, out of place to others.

This larger context, however, offers us some keen insights into the way in which Paul understood the fundamental unifying role that the Eucharist performs in the life of the Christian community. By placing the institution narrative near the end of this particular section of his letter, Paul reminds us that, for the Christian, all questions of moral conduct must ultimately be resolved in the light of Christ's presence in the worshiping community. Paul saw no strict division in his teaching between morality and spirituality; for him, the two were so deeply intertwined that to separate them would do grave damage to the body of Christ, the church. For this reason, he did all he could to root out such a dichotomy from the minds of those he was seeking to form in the life of the Spirit.

The Eucharist, for Paul, was the center of the Christian community and provided its members with the necessary strength and endurance to overcome other areas of their lives that had weakened and given in to the impulses of the flesh. Division in the eucharistic assembly was thus a clear sign that the community was veering away from the love of Christ. Only by restoring that intrinsic unity to the life of the community would there be any hope for the other external divisions to be bound up and eventually healed.

Paul's Institution Narrative: The Immediate Context

More immediately, Paul places his institution narrative (1 Cor 11:23–25) in the center of an exhortation to the community of Corinth about the way they should conduct themselves at the Eucharist (1 Cor 11:17–34). In the section prior to the institution narrative (1 Cor 11:17–22), he details what he has heard about the division and unrest in their eucharistic assembly. In the section that follows the institution narrative (1 Cor 11:26–37), he interprets the meaning of Jesus' action for the life of the believing community and offers some concrete ways of restoring unity to the church. A closer look at the institution narrative and its immediate context reveals a number of important insights.

1. Paul introduces his presentation of the institution narrative with a warning to the community at Corinth:

Now in the following instructions I do not commend you, because when you come together it is not for the better but for the worse. For, to begin with, when you come together as a church, I hear that there are divisions among you; and to some extent I believe it. Indeed, there have to be factions among you, for only so will it become clear who among you are genuine. When you come together, it is not really to eat the Lord's supper. For when the time comes to eat, each of you goes ahead with your own supper, and one goes hungry and another becomes drunk. What! Do you not have homes to eat and drink in? Or do you show contempt for the church of God and humiliate those who have nothing? What should I say to you? Should I commend you? In this matter I do not commend you! (1 Cor 11:17–22)

To understand this section, it is important to remember that the church at Corinth followed the common early Christian practice of celebrating the Eucharist in the context of a fraternal meal (i.e., an *agape* service), what Paul refers to as "the Lord's supper" (v. 20). This meal was a regular feature of early Christian worship and was phased out only when the number of converts became too big to make it practical. The situation in Corinth points to some of the tensions that developed within the community as a result of the practice.

These strained relations stemmed, at least in part, from a lack of charity on the part of richer members toward the poorer ones. Although the majority of the Corinthian Christians came from the lower classes of society, the community's growing numbers necessitated a large gathering place where the worship celebration could take place. The richer members of the community offered their homes for this purpose. Many of them, however, supplied food and drink for their particular group but refused to share what they had with others (v. 19). Some ate hastily so that there would be nothing left to share with those who came a bit late and with nothing to eat. Some even overindulged in the food and drink placed before them, while many of the poorer members of the community were left with nothing. For Paul, such ill-mannered, preferential treatment went entirely against the very meaning of the Christian message. The eucharistic celebration was meant to foster unity, not division. In it the values of Christ, and not the world, were to guide the members of the community in their relations with one another.

2. In response to these abuses, Paul reminds the Corinthians of what he had received and had faithfully passed on to them concerning the institution of the Eucharist:

> I received from the Lord what I also handed on to you, that the Lord Jesus on the night when he was betrayed took a loaf of bread, and when he had given thanks, he broke it and said, "This is my body that is for you. Do this in remembrance of me." In the same way he took the cup also, after supper, saying, "This cup is the new covenant in my blood. Do this, as often as you drink it, in remembrance of me." (1 Cor 11:23–25)

As I stated earlier, Paul's description bears marked similarities to the account in the Gospel of Luke and probably represents the apostolic tradition as it was preserved and handed down in the church at Antioch, the local community in which he himself had worshiped and that had commissioned him for his missionary journeys. This possibility does not necessarily contradict Paul's own claim that he has handed on only what he has received from the Lord. After all, one of the fundamental truths of the gospel he preached was Christ's ongoing presence in the community of members known as his body, the church. For Paul, to receive the apostolic tradition through the mediation of the Christian community was tantamount to receiving it from the Lord himself. In passing on the tradition to the believers at Corinth, he was acting in the name of the Lord and must guarantee that no factions or heresies will distort its true meaning.

Note also the simplicity of the account. The eucharistic action is described as nothing more than a sharing of simple bread and wine. For Paul, the fraternal meal (or *agape*) is not a central feature of the eucharistic celebration. He emphasizes this in his remarks to the Corinthians by focusing only on the essentials of what he has received and faithfully taught them.

3. It is only after he reminds the Corinthians of what he had handed down to them that he provides them with a proper interpretation of its meaning and offers them some concrete suggestions for avoiding any future problems:

> For as often as you eat this bread and drink the cup, you proclaim the Lord's death until he comes. Whoever, therefore, eats the bread or

drinks the cup of the Lord in an unworthy manner will be answerable for the body and blood of the Lord. Examine yourselves, and only then eat of the bread and drink of the cup. For all who eat and drink without discerning the body, eat and drink judgment against themselves. For this reason many of you are weak and ill, and some have died. But if we judged ourselves, we would not be judged. But when we are judged by the Lord, we are disciplined so that we may not be condemned along with the world. So then, my brothers and sisters, when you come together to eat, wait for one another. If you are hungry, eat at home, so that when you come together, it will not be for your condemnation. About the other things I will give instructions when I come. (1 Cor 11:26–34)

In this section of the presentation, the three basic elements of Pauline teaching concerning the Eucharist come to the fore. In the first place, the eucharistic action is a proclamation of the death of the Lord Jesus. This sacrificial dimension comes directly from words of Jesus describing the cup as the "new covenant" in his blood, a reference to the ancient practice of spilling the blood of sacrificial animals to both seal and renew a sacred bond between God and human beings. The Lord's Supper, for Paul, is a proclamation of Jesus' sacrificial offering. His blood was shed on the cross so that a new covenant between God and humanity could be established for all time. To eat the body and to drink the blood of the Lord is to affirm one's faith in Christ's sacrificial death for the sins of the world. It is a proclamation of a new bond between the human and the divine, one that cannot be broken—not even by death itself.

In the second place, the eucharistic action actually brings about the presence of Jesus in the bread and wine itself as well as in the believing community. Not to recognize Jesus in the body is to bring judgment upon oneself. Paul reprimands the Corinth community because their divisive actions toward their own brothers and sisters in the Lord reveal a distorted understanding of their eucharistic worship. To treat fellow Christians in such an irreverent way is to act in similar fashion toward the Lord himself. For Paul, the close bond between the presence of Christ in the bread and wine and the presence of Christ in the believing community is something to be carefully guarded and deeply cherished. It is for this reason that he is so deeply concerned that the eucharistic assembly should be imbued with a spirit of generosity and heartfelt love.

Finally, the eucharistic action points to the eschatological banquet in the kingdom that is to come. The Eucharist, for Paul, takes place in the present, looks to the past, but is intrinsically directed toward the fulfillment of Christ's promises that will come about at his Parousia or Second Coming. It is for this reason that he reminds the Corinthians that to eat the bread and to drink from the cup of the Lord is to proclaim his death "until he comes" (v. 26). This eschatological orientation of the eucharistic action reminds the believing community that its present, time-bound existence will one day overflow into the eternal fullness of God's endearing love. The coming of the Lord Jesus is heralded in by the eucharistic action of the believing community, which looks with expectant hope for the definitive rule of God's reign in the hearts of humankind.

One Bread, One Body

Earlier in this letter, Paul gives the Corinthians an apt summary of his eucharistic theology: "The cup of blessing that we bless, is it not a sharing in the blood of Christ? The bread that we break, is it not a sharing in the body of Christ? Because there is one bread, we who are many are one body, for we all partake of the one bread" (1 Cor 10:16–17). Here, the dimensions of sacrifice, presence, and eschatology that are so prevalent in Paul's eucharistic teaching converge into the unity of Christ's body, the church.

Those who eat the bread and drink from the cup of the Lord's table share in the reality of his sacrificial death, are incorporated into the living presence of his body, the church, and anticipate an even deeper participation in his Spirit in the kingdom that is to come. For Paul, the unity of the community of believers is the visible sign of Christ's active presence in its midst. To disrupt that unity for a selfish or contrary purpose is to work against the Spirit of Christ himself, who otherwise blesses the community with a variety of gifts and charisms to help its members develop and mature (see 1 Cor 12:1–31).

Unity in belief and liturgical practice is thus a fundamental *sine qua non* of a vibrant Christian community. It uses the great variety of gifts and talents within the community for the good of the whole. Lack of unity, by way of contrast, generally disrupts the movement of the Spirit within the community and its members and hinders its missionary witness to the world beyond. It does so by setting one member of the body against the other, thus preventing them from working together for the sake of the kingdom. By using the eucharistic imagery of the one cup of blessing and the one loaf, Paul both affirms the unity in Christ's body as an underlying reality and presents it as a goal to be constantly striven for. When seen in this light, the unity of the believing community is a reality effected by Christ by virtue of his sacrificial death and continuously sought by his disciples in anticipation of his return.

This "already-but-not-yet" quality of the unity present in Christ's body is reflected in the eucharistic celebration itself and is best understood when viewed in the light of the threefold dimensions of Paul's eucharistic teaching described above. For Paul, the Eucharist is not merely a remembrance of a past event, but a present reality that deeply effects the believing community and carries it patiently toward its ultimate term in the glory of the risen Christ. To celebrate the Eucharist is to proclaim the death of the Lord Jesus until he comes again in glory.

Conclusion

When writing to the church at Corinth Paul is keenly aware of it being a divided community. He deals with the contentious groups he finds there by reminding them of the fundamental meaning of the Eucharist and of its absolute necessity for the healthy and well-ordered life of the community. Through this one central focus, he exhorts the members of the church at Corinth to let go of the prejudices that separate them and to allow the unifying force of the Eucharist to draw them more deeply into the transforming love of Christ. This love pours out of the community's liturgical worship and has the remarkable power of changing its members' relationships for the better.

Although the issues may not be the same as those that divided the church at Corinth, a similar dynamic is often at work in many of our present faith communities. We are often burdened by divisive tensions that weigh us down and prevent us from giving witness to the vibrant presence of the gospel message in our lives. Whatever the cause of such divisions (e.g., personality clashes, divergent theological opinions, questions of power and authority), we need to examine ourselves to see if our actions correspond to what we profess when we participate in the Eucharist and receive the body and blood of Christ (see 1 Cor 11:28–29). Deep dissension within a local community is nearly always a sign that the body of Christ is not receiving the reverence and respect it deserves. The presences of Christ in the Eucharist and in his body, the church, are so deeply intertwined that divisions within the community can only be accounted for by a failure to recognize the true significance of the action of Christ taking place in the Eucharist. The gap between what the Eucharist effects and how community members behave toward one another has no other feasible explanation.

To one extent or another, every Christian community has experienced its share of internal division and disrupting, factious behavior. The eschatological dimension of the eucharistic celebration itself reminds us that the church's pilgrimage through time is not yet over and that, as long as it continues, a gap is almost sure to exist between the ideals we profess and the concrete behavior we exhibit in our lives. When seen in this light, the key question that we must face when dealing with such internal tensions is whether the gap between faith and practice in our daily life is progressively increasing or decreasing. Our response to this question will have a great influence on how we perceive ourselves as a faith community and what concrete steps we can take to insure our faithfulness to the gospel and a life of ongoing conversion.

Reflection Questions

• Are there any divisions in the Christian community to which you belong? If so, what seems to be their source? How long have they been going on?

• How has the community attempted to resolve these divisions and bring about a healing?

• How do these individuals or groups relate during the Eucharist? Do they simply ignore each other? Do they pretend as though the tensions do not exist? Do they extend a hand of peace to each other?

• If the Eucharist is a sign of unity, in what ways does its celebration encourage the members of your community to put aside their differences? Can you think of any concrete steps that could help the process along?

Living Members

The Body of Believers

For just as the body is one and has many members, and all the members of the body, though many, are one body, so it is with Christ. For in the one Spirit we were all baptized into one body—Jews or Greeks, slaves or free—and we were all made to drink of one Spirit. (1 Cor 12:12–13)

If you had to go through life without a part of your body, which part would you choose? Answering a question like this is more difficult than one might think. Our bodies are so important to us that few of us would readily give up any part of it unless we absolutely had to. I know I wouldn't.

A person's self-image is intimately tied to his or her experience of embodiment. We experience life through our bodily senses, processing our thoughts and emotions through sensations that come to us through what we hear, see, touch, taste, and smell. "Faith," the apostle Paul tells us, "comes from what is heard" (Rom 10:17). Christian asceticism has traditionally employed bodily discipline as a means of helping a person draw closer to God. The sacraments themselves engage our bodily senses to mediate God's grace to us in concrete, visible ways.

Jesus of Nazareth was asked not only to give up a part of his body, but all of it. He did so willingly, out of love for us. When instituting the Eucharist he sought to share that love with us as much as he could. The night before he died, he gathered his closest disciples around him and, in a final parting gesture, shared bread and wine with them, saying, "This is my body…This is my blood." These words were carefully chosen and freely shared. They embody Jesus and his mission—all that he lived and died for. Through them he invites us to become a part of him. He gives up his body and makes it available to us in this way so that we can live in him and he in us.

When we eat his body and drink his blood, we become intimately tied to Jesus. We become, one might say, a part of his own self-image. For this reason, the Eucharist has special significance for the community of believers. It gives us a living encounter with the risen Lord and forges bonds of communion among the various members of his body.

This twofold dynamic comes through most clearly in Paul's first letter to the Corinthians. His teaching in this letter affirms the action of Christ in the breaking of the bread by the believing community. This action flows from the living, dynamic presence of Christ in the midst of his followers. From there it extends to the gifts and talents of each member, which are used for building up the body and the proclamation of the gospel.

Diverse Unities

As we saw in the last chapter, Paul preserves the earliest recorded version of the Last Supper (1 Cor 11:23–25). His interpretation of what he has received from the Lord and handed on to the fledgling church at Corinth delves deeply into the very meaning of the community of faith. The Eucharist, for Paul, constitutes the body of Christ, the church. Without it, there would be nothing to bind us together and make us one (see 1 Cor 10:16–17). This unity stems from the community's sharing in the Lord's death and its belief in his imminent return: "For as often as you eat this bread and drink the cup, you proclaim the Lord's death until he comes" (1 Cor 11:26).

For Paul, the unity of the community of believers stems from their breaking bread together. This common ritual symbolizes the nature of right relationship within community, and also brings it about. These right relationships are based on a notion of unity and diversity and come from the juxtaposition in his teaching of the imagery of "loaf" and "body." This juxtaposition comes from the words of Jesus himself in the words of institution: "This is my body that is for you. Do this in remembrance of me" (1 Cor 11:24).

Two different types of unity are implied in this important juxtaposition. On the one hand there is the homogeneity of the one loaf that comes through a long process of harvesting, grinding, kneading, and baking. This kind of unity involves a "transformation through breakdown," of a sort not unlike what Jesus underwent through his passion and death. When identifying the loaf of bread with his body, Jesus is referring to the suffering that he himself will shortly undergo. On the other hand, there is the complex, organic unity of the body that comes through the re-creative processes of human biological development. This kind of unity involves a "transformation through nourishment and growth," of a sort that Jesus himself underwent in the womb of his mother and throughout his life on earth. When identifying the loaf of bread with his body, he is referring to the dynamism of his life that he wishes to impart to his disciples.

These two very different types of unity come together in the act of Christ's breaking bread with his disciples. Through this communal act of table fellowship, the type of unity depicted in the imagery of "the one loaf" comes into contact with the type of unity presented in the imagery of "the one body." Through the eucharistic action of eating and drinking, in other words, the process of transformation "through breakdown" becomes closely intertwined with, almost inseparable from, that of "nourishment and growth." Both are essential to the way the eucharistic action represents the Christ event: the former embraces the downward chaotic movement of Christ's passion and death; the latter, the upward, re-creative movement of his resurrection, ascension, and return in glory. Paul capitalizes on this juxtaposition of imagery and makes it the basis of his doctrine of the church as the body of Christ.

The Body of Christ

If Jesus is responsible for juxtaposing the imagery of bread and body when he ate with his disciples for the last time, it was Paul who drew out the implications of this action for the community of believers. The Last Supper was a symbolic action that effected what it signified. It not only pointed back to Jesus' baptism, with which it encompassed the whole of his public ministry, but also forward to the events of his passion, death, and resurrection. Paul's great insight was to see the significance of this eucharistic action for the community of faith. Although he did not invent the analogy of the body to describe the functioning of human society, his application of this model to the Eucharist made explicit what was already implicit in Jesus' symbolic action. The resulting doctrine had strong ramifications for the church's self-understanding.

Paul's teaching occurs in many places in his letters, but is most succinctly stated in 1 Corinthians chapter 12. The text reads:

(12) For just as the body is one and has many members, and all the members of the body, though many, are one body, so it is with Christ. (13) For in the one Spirit we were all baptized into one body—Jews or Greeks, slaves or free—and we were all made to drink of one Spirit. (14) Indeed, the body does not consist of one member but of many. (15) If the foot would say, "Because I am not a hand, I do not belong to the body," that would not make it any less a part of the body. (16) And if the ear would say, "Because I am not an eye, I do not belong to the body," that would not make it any less a part of the body. (17) If the whole body were an eye, where would the hearing be? If the whole body were hearing, where would the sense of smell be? (18) But as it is, God arranged the members in the body, each one of them, as he chose. (19) If all were a single member, where would the body be? (20) As it is, there are many members, yet one body. (21) The eye cannot say to the hand, "I have no need of you," nor again the head to the feet, "I have no need of you." (22) On the contrary, the members of the body that seem to be weaker are indispensable, (23) and those members of the body that we think less honorable we clothe with greater honor, and our less respectable members are treated with greater respect; (24) whereas our more respectable members do not need this. But God has so arranged the body, giving the greater honor to the inferior member, (25) that there may be no dissension within the body, but the members may have the same care for one another. (26) If one member suffers, all suffer together with it; if one member is honored, all rejoice together with it. (1 Cor 12:12–26)

It bears noting that Paul associates this teaching with both baptism and the Eucharist (v. 13). Through baptism, a person is incorporated into the glorified, risen body of Christ and is able to eat and drink worthily at the table of the Lord. These sacramental actions were instituted at the beginning and end of Jesus' public ministry and can be taken to encompass both his message and the consequences flowing from it. It is in this sense that, for Paul, a person is baptized into Jesus' death and resurrection and partakes of his body and blood.

Paul applies this analogy of the body to the community of believers: "Now you are the body of Christ and individually members of it" (1 Cor 12:27). He then highlights the various ministries of this one body: "God has appointed in the church first apostles, second prophets, third teachers; then deeds of power, then gifts of healing, forms of assistance, forms of leadership, various kinds of tongues" (1 Cor 12:28). Delineating the various kinds of ministry in the church gives him the opportunity to circle back to his earlier line of argument: "Are all apostles? Are all prophets? Are all teachers? Do all work miracles? Do all possess gifts of healing? Do all speak in tongues? Do all interpret?" (1 Cor 12:29–30).

Paul ends his treatment of the body of Christ by exhorting the members of the church at Corinth to set their hearts on the higher gifts, the greatest of which is love. It is the Spirit of love that preserves the church's unity and enables it to preserve the harmony of ministries and gifts. This love is precisely what is celebrated at the Eucharist, which at that time in Corinth was celebrated in the context of a fellowship meal known as the *agape* feast.

A Variety of Interpretations

A variety of interpretations have been given to Paul's doctrine of the body of Christ. On one end of the spectrum it is thought to be merely a metaphor. This position assigns nothing but literary value to the teaching. The church is considered the "body of Christ" only in a figurative sense. It asserts that Christ and his Spirit inspire the community of believers to act in a certain way in much the same way that a good poem affects its readers. This view does not accept the possibility that Christ himself is the principal agent in the affairs of the community and that the church, as his body, is in some way a real, concrete extension on earth of his glorified divine and human person.

On the other end of the spectrum is what might be termed the realist position. This approach asserts the actual identity of the church with the transfigured body of the risen Lord. According to this perspective, the church and its members are one with Christ, not merely by virtue of spirit and inspiration, but in actual fact. Here, the glorified Christ is thought to act in and through the members of the church. They are his body in an absolute, not a figurative sense. One version of this approach collapses the body of the transfigured Lord into the visible church so that he can only act through it and not apart from it. Another version recognizes the members of the church as integral parts of Christ's transfigured body, but is not willing to admit a strict one to one correspondence between them. In either case, the church and its members are considered vital, organic components of Christ's glorified body.

Between these two extremes lies the sacramental position. According to this perspective, calling the church the body of Christ involves a certain likeness and difference with its primary referent. Although it cannot be univocally identified with Christ's glorified body, it is much more than a mere figurative description. To refer to the church in this way is to affirm the real presence of Christ in the believing community. That presence, however, functions by way of both positive and negative assertion. Christ's enduring presence in the church is real but not complete. The "already-but-not-yet" texture of the affirmation accentuates the eschatological nature of the church and its radical orientation toward the fullness of the kingdom. For this reason, Paul's doctrine of the church as the body of Christ is perhaps best understood in a sacramental sense, and it is here where its deep connection with the eucharistic action comes to the fore.

In later centuries, scholastic theologians would discuss the sacraments in terms of its "outward sign" (*sacramentum tantum*), its "inner movement of grace" (*res sacramenti*), and an "intermediary element between the two" (*res et sacramentum*). When applied to the Eucharist, the "outward signs" of the sacrament are the bread and wine; the "inner movement of grace" is the help of the Holy Spirit given through the sacrament; and the "intermediate element between the two" is the real presence of the risen Lord in the eucharistic species. When considered in this sacramental sense, the "outward signs" of the church refer to the various members of the believing community; the "inner movement of grace" to the abiding life of the Holy Spirit in their hearts; and the "intermediate elements between the two" to the real but mysterious presence of the risen Lord in their midst.

The sacramental continuum, moreover, of Christ as the "sacrament of God," the church as the "sacrament of Christ," and the sacraments as "sacraments of the church" would even give the understanding of the church as the "body of Christ" a certain priority over the presence of Christ in the Eucharist. The Eucharist, one might say, both constitutes the church and is constituted by it. As the source and summit of the church's life, it gives visible expression to a reality already present in its members and offers them a way to bring their yearnings for the fullness of the messianic banquet to the fore.

Observations

The above insights into the meaning of Paul's teaching on the church as the body of Christ affirm its importance for the growing self-understanding of the believing community and give rise to a number of interesting remarks.

1. To begin with, Paul develops his teaching in a response to a divided church at Corinth. Strong tensions existed within the community over such issues as eating meat offered to idols (1 Cor 10:14–22), the role of women at worship (1 Cor 11: 2–16), and proper comportment during the eucharistic feast (1 Cor 11:17–22). Paul points to the Eucharist as the concrete expression of harmony within the community of believers. That harmony is rooted in an organic concept of unity that, at one and the same time, allows for both the radical equality of the members and a division of ministries within the church.

2. Because of the abuses taking place during the *agape* service (1 Cor 11:17–22), it remains unclear if Paul wishes to merely reform or do away entirely with the meal during which the Eucharist took place. Whatever his intentions, the growth of Christianity in the Hellenic world would eventually make an entire meal impractical for the eucharistic service. Larger numbers and places of worship would eventually require a slimmed down version of the Last Supper, one that would focus on the essentials, while retaining the semblance of a meal.

3. The developing understanding of the Eucharist as a sacrificial meal

would eventually cause the table upon which it was celebrated to also serve as an altar. This juxtaposition of functions reflects what was said earlier about "transformation through breakdown" and "transformation through nourishment and growth." Treating the Eucharist as a banquet promotes the kind of unity brought about through "transformation through nourishment and growth." Treating it as a sacrifice, however, promotes the kind of unity brought about through "transformation through breakdown." The juxtaposition of the banquet and sacrificial understandings of the Eucharist promotes a dynamic understanding of unity and invites those who participate to look beyond appearances and to focus on what binds them to Christ and to one another.

4. The benefit of the sacramental understanding of Paul's teaching of the church as the body of Christ stems from its ability to maintain a tension between Christ's ongoing presence and absence. It promotes, at one and the same time, the real presence of Christ in the believing community and the strong anticipation of his awaited return. This "already-but-not-yet" quality steers a middle course between extremes and preserves the important eschatological orientation of the Christian faith. That orientation flows from the very nature of the Christ event into the very life of the community and its rituals of divine worship.

5. Paul's teaching makes explicit what is already implicit in the words of institution. Jesus not only identifies the bread and wine with his body and blood, but also shares them with his disciples. This act of sharing represents a desire to impart to his disciples the very essence of his life and mission. By the eating of his body and blood, the members of the believing community reaffirm the mystery of their baptism in Jesus' paschal mystery. That action confirms them in their dedication to carry on Christ's work in the present. To do that work effectively, they have been gifted to perform a variety of ministries for the building up of the church and the common good of all humanity.

6. When examining Paul's teaching one must be careful to avoid attributing to him concepts and distinctions that were formulated by later thinkers. That is not to say, however, that such tools cannot be used to elicit elements from the Pauline doctrine that remain unclear or are in need of further explanation. The scholastic terminology used in sacramental

theology (e.g., *sacramentum tantum, res tantum, res et sacramentum*) is a case in point. The purpose of their use in this context is not to attribute to Paul distinctions of which he could not possibly have been aware, but to demonstrate the teaching's close affinity with a sacramental outlook and the consequences that flow from such a perspective.

7. The use of the sacramental continuum of Christ as the "sacrament of God," the church as the "sacrament of Christ," and the sacraments as "sacraments of the church" to explain Paul's teaching is yet another example of the use of later theological distinctions to draw out elements of his thought. Again, the goal here is not to attribute to Paul's mind concepts formulated at a later date, but to use these distinctions to present the doctrine of the church as the body of Christ in a light that would be both understandable and relevant for today's believer. The strength of these particular distinctions is that they give a certain priority to the body of Christ, the church, over the body of Christ in the Eucharist, even though the latter effectively predates it. The use of such distinctions argues for the close bond between Christ, his church, and the sacraments and the unity they seek to promote.

These observations in no way exhaust the richness of Paul's teaching on the church as the body of Christ. Together they point to the variety of approaches one can take to the doctrine and to the helpful way in which distinctions formulated at a later date can be used to shed some light on the relevance of the doctrine for today. If nothing else, they should encourage openness to the close bond that this doctrine shares with the Eucharist and the person from whose hands that mystery was first instituted.

Conclusion

Paul's teaching on the church as the body of Christ seeks to preserve the unity of the community of believers in the midst of great diversity. It does so by capitalizing on the juxtaposition of imagery found in the institution narrative of the Eucharist and by extending its significance to the lives of the faithful. In doing so, Paul forges a close, intimate bond between the inner harmony of the community and its celebration of the eucharistic banquet, one that goes to the very heart of the faith and of what it means to live a life of discipleship.

The variety of interpretations given to Paul's teaching reflects a broad spectrum of opinion, ranging anywhere from a figurative, purely metaphorical interpretation of the relationship between Christ's glorified body and the members of the church to a realist affirmation of the identity between the two. A sacramental interpretation of his teaching holds the middle ground between these extremes and offers a way of interpreting Christ's relationship to his followers through an ongoing assertion of his presence and absence in the life of the community. Doing so brings forth the eschatological orientation of the Christian community and roots it in the "already-but-not-yet" quality of the eucharistic action.

In the final analysis, Paul's teaching on the church as the body of Christ represents an attempt to draw out the full implications of Jesus' last meal with his disciples for the wider community of faith. The consequences of this teaching should not be underestimated. Through the eucharistic action, we affirm Christ's presence in our midst and anticipate the fullness of the kingdom to come. In the meantime, we break bread together to express the unity of our faith and to commit ourselves to carry on the mission that Christ himself began.

Reflection Questions

• What does the doctrine of the church as the body of Christ mean to you? Do you interpret it in a spiritual, realistic, or a sacramental sense? Can you think of any other way to look at it?

• Have you ever had an experience of "transformation through breakdown" or "transformation through nourishment"? Which of the two do you associate most with your experience of church? Are they in any way juxtaposed in your experience?

• Does it make sense to you to speak of the church as the sacrament of Christ? What consequences does such an approach have for your understanding of the Eucharist?

• Is Christ's presence or absence more prevalent in your experience of church? Does the tension between the two make you feel hopeful or ill-at-ease? In what way is this tension present in your celebration of the Eucharist?

Conclusion

One of the most interesting properties of a finely cut diamond is that it reflects light differently with each change of perspective. Shine the sun's light on it from a slightly different angle and the sparkling glitter it reflects will change accordingly. Much the same can be said for the Eucharist. Down through the centuries its significance for Christians, while always central, has reflected the various needs and concerns that they have brought to it. As a result, the Eucharist has remained a dynamic rather than a static presence in the life of the believing community.

Throughout this book we have used the image of a finely cut diamond as a metaphor for understanding the meaning of the Eucharist for the early Christian community. We have seen how the breaking of the bread was a central concern of the New Testament writers and how they embedded it in their writings in a variety of ways. While none of these scriptural accounts fully exhausts the meaning of the Eucharist, their cumulative effect offers us a good idea of how the early Christians understood this sacramental mystery and were inspired and even empowered by it.

What was the result of this influence? —Discipleship, faith, prayer, celebration, healing, community, mystery, service. These are just some of the many facets reflected in the New Testament writings on the Eucharist. Each of these themes reflects the light of the gospel in a special way and encourages us to open our hearts to the message of God's redeeming love, which it inspires. Taken together, they remind us of what Christians do and are called to become. They reveal to us Christ's dream for us and incite us to make these fundamental values of the kingdom thoroughly our own.

There is no other way to make these values our own than by simply falling on our knees and asking the Lord for help. The Eucharist is the prayer of Christ's body, the church. It reflects the divine light and directs it into our hearts through, with, and in Christ. Through the Eucharist, our prayers become those of Jesus, our Lord. When we gather to break bread together, Jesus enters our midst and burns within our hearts. As he prays to the Father, our prayers become uniquely joined with his. His Spirit yearns within us, and our spirits yearn within him. The Eucharist points to the kingdom and, be it but for a short period of time, also makes it present.

Diamonds, we should remember, also number among the hardest and most enduring of precious stones. Made from coal when it is subjected to great pressures deep within the earth, they cut through the heaviest of metals and are noted for their ability to endure a very high intensity of heat. In a similar fashion, the Eucharist was forged in the flaming furnace of Christ's paschal mystery and receives its transforming beauty from the radiance of his resurrection. For this reason, it is the greatest and most enduring act of Christian worship. Through it, we come in contact with the passion, death, and resurrection of Jesus.

When we receive the Eucharist, Jesus' story becomes our own, and ours his. From it we receive insight into our call and sustenance for our journey. From it we receive light for guidance and the grace to endure. Without the Eucharist, there would be no Good News, no apostolic witness, no New Testament, no Christian community. The Eucharist is like a multifaceted diamond—and so very much more. It is mystery. It is divine love. It is eternal life. It is manna from heaven. It is living bread. It is real food and real drink. It is our immortal diamond, all at once what Christ is and what we can and will become, both now and always—just for the asking.